THE MANAGER'S
ANSWER
BOOK

THE MANAGER'S ANSWER BOOK

Powerful Tools to Build Trust and
Teams, Maximize Your Impact and
Influence, and Respond to Challenges

**BARBARA MITCHELL
AND CORNELIA GAMLEM**

CAREER
PRESS

This edition first published in 2018 by Career Press, an imprint of
Red Wheel/Weiser, LLC
With offices at: 65 Parker Street, Suite 7
Newburyport, MA 01950
www.redwheelweiser.com
www.careerpress.com

ISBN: 978-163265-141-9
Library of Congress Cataloging-in-Publication Data
available upon request.

Cover design by Rob Johnson/Toprotype
Interior by PerfecType, Nashville, Tennesee
Typeset in Stempel Garamond LT Std

Printed in Canada
MAR
10 9 8 7 6 5 4 3 2 1

To all the great managers we've worked with
throughout our careers!

ACKNOWLEDGMENTS

WRITING A BOOK is a journey and throughout our careers, we have encountered situations and had experiences that we have been able to incorporate into this book. There have also been many managers with whom we were able to share advice and who, in turn, shared their knowledge with us. Thanks to all of you who inspired many of the questions and answers in this book.

There are certain people to whom we are especially grateful for their help in writing *The Manager's Answer Book*. First, thanks to Ralph Kidder for sharing your experiences as a CFO and your insights on managing many of the staff functions in organizations. Rich Cohrs, you generously provided us with your observations from years of working with and leading Corporate Communications. Erik Gamlem, we greatly appreciate your thoughts and experiences regarding what employees wish a new manager would do. Marna Hayden, you always have great insights, and we appreciated your thoughts about diversity and corporate manners. Beth Gilley, we are grateful for the excellent information about Employee Assistance Programs you've provided us over the years. Jennifer Whitcomb, you remain our go-to person for questions about coaching employees. And Steve Dorfman, thanks for sharing your experiences and insights over the years about the customer experience.

Our "writing life" has also been a journey, and there are many people who have supported us along the way. At the top of the list is Marilyn Allen, our literary agent, for responding to our endless questions and ideas. You're a wonderful coach and advocate who gives us great advice and encouragement to want to keep writing. The staff at

Career Press continues to present us with ideas and believe in us. We appreciate all your support, especially from the editors with whom we have worked and for putting us in the hands of good public relations professionals who get us great exposure.

We cannot forget the booksellers who see the value of our books and display them on their shelves of both brick-and-mortar and virtual stores. One of those booksellers deserves special recognition. Thanks to Cal Hunt, manager of the business book section of Barnes & Noble on Fifth Avenue in New York, New York, for displaying *The Big Book of HR* as a top pick in business books!

Finally, we want to acknowledge you, our readers. Leaders can't lead without followers. Authors can't write without readers. Thank you.

CONTENTS

Introduction: How to Use This Book 11

Section 1: You're a New Manager, Now What? 15

Section 2: Developing Your Management Skills 47

Section 3: Building and Managing Your Team 79

Section 4: Creating Your Personal Brand 111

Section 5: Managing Up, Down, and Around 135

Section 6: Avoiding Potential Land Mines 161

Section 7: Recognizing Legal Pitfalls 185

Notes 199

Resources 201

Glossary of Management and Business Terms 203

About the Authors 221

INTRODUCTION: HOW TO USE THIS BOOK

CONGRATULATIONS, YOU'RE A manager! You may be a new manager and you're encountering issues for the first time. You may be an experienced manager, but this situation has never come up before. You may be new to the company, organization, or industry, and things are done differently.

Of course you have expertise in the field you're managing, but what about everything else? There's so much more to know. Whether you're a new or seasoned manager, your responsibilities can be overwhelming at times. There are days and new situations that leave you feeling vulnerable. You don't know where to start or even what to ask! Do you fly by the seat of your pants, take an educated guess, or just throw up your hands and give up? No manager should feel that isolated or vulnerable.

That's where *The Manager's Answer Book* can help. In question-and-answer format, this easy-to-use guide provides information on many aspects of managing. You will find guidance on the following:

- **You're a New Manager, Now What?** Getting started as a manager, either a first-time manager or a manager in a new organization, can be daunting. This section covers issues such as following in the footsteps of a great or not-so-great predecessor, moving from peer to manager, developing relationships, metrics and budgets, managing projects and resources, and much more.
- **Developing Your Management Skills.** Beyond the knowledge and expertise in your field, being a manager

requires skill. You may already possess good communication skills, including storytelling, or be a master at time management. However, to be effective as a manager, you need to delegate, motivate, coach and counsel, mediate, negotiate, and facilitate, all topics included in the section—and then some.

- **Building and Managing Your Team.** People management is an important part of your job. From hiring to firing and everything in between—such as onboarding employees, setting goals and expectations, providing feedback, rewards, recognition, and retention—this section covers these and other issues you need to know about being an effective leader of people.

- **Creating Your Personal Brand.** Image and credibility are important for you and your team, and this extends beyond your physical looks and appearance. This section covers many best management practices: building trust, setting examples through words and actions, ethics and integrity, vulnerability, and emotional intelligence. It includes tips on these and other topics to help you understand why your brand is important.

- **Managing Up, Down, and Around.** Managing doesn't stop with your own team. You have to understand how the rest of the organization functions to be effective and this section provides many of those insights as well as guidance on managing people and situations outside your scope of authority.

- **Avoiding Potential Land Mines.** It could be easy to get caught in situations that could backfire or explode—conflict and change and risk, oh my! Then there's managing remote workers, telecommuters, and generations, as well as understanding external requirements, to name a few more.

- **Recognizing Legal Pitfalls.** Just when you thought everything was covered, there's the myriad of laws and regulations. You can find insights on situations that you could likely face.

The information provided in *The Manager's Answer Book* is at times general in nature. Policies, processes, and protocols will vary from organization to organization and from industry to industry. Academia and non-profits may have different procedures and protocols than organizations in industries such as manufacturing, healthcare, or government contracting. The size of the organization also affects how things get done and the resources available. We will often suggest that you consult with your legal or human resources support, recognizing that support may be an internal department or an external resource. It's important that you take the time to learn how things are accomplished in your organization.

The Manager's Answer Book can help any manager stay informed and avoid unknowingly tripping over a new situation. It provides insights into many situations and issues that managers face outside their own area of expertise. It's a natural complement to *The Big Book of HR*.

You're a New Manager, Now What?

CONGRATULATIONS! THIS IS an exciting time in your career, but you probably have a lot of questions and not a lot of answers as you take on new responsibilities. Here's a tip as you get started: You've hopefully had a couple of good managers in your career, so think about what they did that worked for you and use that insight to guide you along with the answers in this section.

Question: My predecessor was a manager who was held in high esteem by everyone—her staff, her peers, and the leadership. I certainly don't want to alienate the employees, but I'm not her and will likely have a different style. Any advice for starting on a positive note with my staff?

Answer: If your predecessor was highly regarded, there are probably many reasons for it. I would guess that a competent staff is one of the top reasons. Successful managers hire good staff—people who are good at what they do. As you start in your new job, you will want to make getting to know your staff a top priority. Learn what it is that they do and what expertise each one of them possesses. Trust them with what they are doing. In many cases, they have probably been doing it for a long time, either within your organization or elsewhere.

Your team members also possess a great deal of institutional knowledge. If they've been with the organization for a while, that knowledge can even be greater than the knowledge of the person who hired you. Yes, you may be able to tap into your peer network for this, but they will not necessarily know how to apply that knowledge to your department or team's work. Your staff will, and you will need to leverage the knowledge they bring.

Don't micromanage the staff. Yes, you may be trying to get a better understanding of what they do and contribute. However, if you're initially asking for a great deal of information or status reports, explain to them it's because you're trying to learn—to gain a greater understand of what they do—and that it won't continue indefinitely. Focus on their results.

Don't reallocate work and responsibilities arbitrarily. At some point, as you get to know what each staff member's workload is, it may be necessary to do so. However, get input—from all those affected. Also, don't arbitrarily change procedures and processes. Get suggestions from the staff. After all, they are the ones performing the work. Keep in mind that what may have worked in your former organization may not work in the new organization. In fact, they may have tried something you are proposing in the past and it failed to work. Listen to them. Making arbitrary changes can have the effect of demoralizing and demotivating the staff.

Recognize and respect the professional relationships your staff members have made both inside and outside the organization. They have worked hard at building relationships with peers, the leadership, clients, customers, and service providers. They have built credible, reputations in their professional networks and often within the community. Honor that and don't try to capitalize on it for your personal gain. Once they have gotten a chance to know and trust you better, they will probably be more than happy to introduce you to their network.

Most importantly, give your staff time to adjust to their new leadership. They've experienced a loss and are going through a grieving process. Listen to them and give them time to adjust—along with your respect and trust!

Question: I just accepted a job with a new organization. I'm replacing a manager who is retiring, and he had a number of short-comings that I've heard were not addressed. Apparently, he had an "anything goes" attitude and gave his staff a great deal of freedom. Needless to say, they held him in high regard. The leadership has told me they want me to bring more accountability to the department. Could you give me some pointers about how to approach the staff?

Answer: Wow, this is a challenge. It sounds like the staff was taking advantage of your predecessor's lack of control and might expect that you will maintain the same status quo. That's not to say you should tread lightly, just slowly and deliberately.

Obviously, you want to build rapport with each staff member. Find out from each of them how they perceive their job—their duties and responsibilities. Compare this to any job descriptions and your leadership's understanding of their jobs. This will help you identify any gaps that you need to address.

Be clear with your staff about your expectations—of them and of the department. Let them know this as soon as possible and rein-force your expectations often in discussions with them and in staff meetings. Despite what they may think, employees really do want to know what's expected of them. Don't just tell them what you expect; tell them why you expect it. Provide facts (for example, "We serve the public, so it's important to be punctual and arrive at work on time").

Acknowledge to the team that things will change and be dif-ferent as you all adjust. Solicit their input, especially if you plan to change procedures or protocols. Let them know you will take all of their ideas and opinions under consideration, but ultimately you, in consultation with the leadership, will make any final decisions. This approach will help manage their expectations.

Remind them that all of you are a team and ultimately work for the same organization. Often, individuals in these circumstances perceive that they work for one particular person. In this case, they may think they worked more for your predecessor and less for the organization. Be clear that you all support the organization and its stakeholders, such as clients and customers. Stress that as a manager you have a responsibility to make sure that the stakeholders are being served. Your accountability, and theirs, goes beyond the chain of command.

Put action behind your words. Show them that you are part of the team and that you value the work that each staff member does. Be willing to roll up your sleeves and help with routine tasks if the situation requires it. Offer to help, as a way of better understanding what it is that they do. It will help gain their confidence and trust.

Finally, communicate any changes that need to be made. Explain why the changes are necessary. Give the staff warning before you implement them, but do so in a timely manner. This will increase your credibility with them.

Remember that this is an adjustment period and that it's a process. Give your staff the time to adjust while holding them accountable.

Question: My new job means I am managing former peers and friends. In addition to assigning work and monitoring progress on projects, I will be evaluating their performance. Are there some ways to let them know that things have changed and that we must work together differently?

Answer: You've got some hard work ahead of you. It isn't easy to change hats and manage people you consider to be your friends, but it's certainly possible to successfully move from peer to boss—and it starts as soon as the announcement is made that you're now in charge.

Hopefully, your organization has selected you for this role because you've exhibited the qualities a good manager needs to have, including the ability to motivate others, good delegation skills, and excellent communication skills. If you need to refresh your skills, there are lots of books, podcasts, YouTube videos, and blogs available to help you hit the ground running.

Your first meeting with your team is critical, but you may want to wait a day or two for the news to settle before you jump in with both feet. Let people adjust to the fact that you are now their manager before you let your team know what is expected of them. They need to hear that you will support them in any way possible and will get out of their way so they can do the jobs they were hired for. What makes your situation somewhat uneasy is that you have some personal relationships with certain people, and they know you in a way, perhaps, that most people don't know their bosses.

Meet one-on-one with each person who reports to you and clarify your expectations. Let them know your goals for the department and how you see them contributing to its success. Clearly spell out that you value each person and their contributions to the organization while reminding them that you now have a different role to play.

In these conversations, be professional and open to hearing your team members' ideas. Acknowledge that you will be holding them accountable for their work and that you will support them in any way possible. Ask them to express any concerns they have, and respond to those concerns. Make a commitment to each person that you will be fair and honest in all your dealings with them.

This is the time to be clear about another aspect of your new role. Now that you're responsible for the team's performance, you have lots of additional responsibilities and many meetings to attend so you probably won't be as available as you once were for lunches or after-work activities. You certainly don't want to cut off all informal contact with your team—just back off a bit from the socialization.

There may be people who can't handle the new relationship and you will have to make hard decisions—but that's what managers do. Just keep in mind that your responsibility is to the team and to the success of the organization. If you need help, ask your HR support. And if you have a mentor, this is a perfect time to ask for guidance as you manage your new responsibilities and your team.

Question: I'm settling into my new role managing my department and I'm developing a good rapport with my team. However, I'm not sure that's enough. What else should I be doing?

Answer: A big challenge for a new manager, whether you're new to the role or new to the organization, is fitting in and learning how things get done. Beyond understanding the organization, which is important, you have to develop political savvy. You need to begin by learning the organization—its structure and complexity. Some organizations have a traditional hierarchical structure; some are flatter or have a matrix structure with people often working on cross-functional teams. The structure is going to affect how information flows, and understanding this is critical, so learn it early. Equally important, determine who the gatekeepers of the information are—those individuals who control the flow of information. Also, pay attention to how ideas flow in your organization. Do they flow freely? Do team members have the freedom to either act on good ideas or at least bring them forward?

Practice management by walking around, inside and outside of your department. Be observant and ask questions. Pay attention to the people and the action around you. How is the work being done? What are people saying about your department? Whether the feedback you're getting is positive or negative, don't settle on hearsay. Go to the source to get the best information that you can and invite comments and criticism. You will not be able to make any positive changes unless you understand the changes that need to be made.

Curiosity is one of the most important tools you should be using in your management journey. Curious people are always learning because they're always asking questions, reading up on topics outside their field of expertise, and generally exploring. Being curious and asking questions is a good way to engage other people.

Be curious about what's going on in your organization. Start with finding out what other departments or teams are doing. Not only do you learn about the work, you can learn more about other managers. Be genuine and let them know that you want to hear more about their work and their teams. And listen carefully to what they say!

If you're curious, you're also likely to ask about the challenges your external and internal customers face. It will help you gain a deeper understanding of what's going on in the organization, and what others are facing. It's also a great way to build new relationships!

Question: Now that I'm a manager, someone advised me that I have to be mindful of perception—what other people think of me and what I do. I've always considered myself a straight-forward individual. Do I have to change who I am?

Answer: You've gotten some good advice about being mindful of what others think, but no, it doesn't mean you have to change who you are. Just be aware how you present yourself. People will be watching you—your team, your peers, and your leadership—and all those people will have new expectations of you because of your new role. They are forming opinions based on their interpretations of what they see you doing and saying.

So what, exactly, should you be mindful of as you settle into your new role? Here are some things to consider:

- **Your dress and physical appearance.** Workplaces today have indeed become more casual, so, depending on the industry and the nature of your workplace, you want to dress suitably for your normal workday environment. If your workplace is casual, however, avoid anything outlandish that draws negative attention to you. Any stylist and image consultant will advise you to dress for where your day will take you. If you have meetings outside the office, you may need to forego casual and dress in more traditional business attire. Beyond clothing, don't forget to check the mirror periodically to ensure you're well groomed. You don't want to appear disheveled.
- **Your workspace.** We all have different ways of organizing our work and projects so we can work efficiently. Some people have items in file folders, others in piles. Keep in mind, however, that as people enter your workplace, they will form an impression of you. Will they see a busy manager or chaos? Though some people may like to work at a relatively clear desk, no one expects your workplace to be pristine all the time. Be mindful of keeping things haphazardly cast around your office (boxes or piles of things sitting around the floor, for example). Such a habit will not cast you in the best light.
- **Your language.** It goes without saying that you should use professional language in the workplace. Avoid slang and jargon. You may be used to a looser, less-formal style of communications, which may have been fine in your former environment or role. However, that's not where you are now. Not everyone will "get" that style

of speaking and communicating, or understand that you may be joking if you respond to others with barbs and sarcasm.

- **Your manners.** Beyond table manners, and you should use good ones at business meals, don't forget common sense. When you're introduced to someone, stand if you're sitting. Shake hands or otherwise acknowledge them and learn their name. Repeat their name ("It's nice to meet you, Mary Smith") during the introduction. Be attentive to others. Don't interrupt or finish a person's sentence. Say "please," "thank you," and "excuse me." Be gracious and accept compliments. Be punctual for meetings, but if you're delayed, do you best to get a message to the host. When you arrive, be inconspicuous when you join so you aren't disruptive.

Warren Buffett said, "It takes twenty years to build a reputation and five minutes to ruin it. If you think about that, you'll do things differently."[1]

Question: I am adjusting to my new managerial responsibilities but am struggling with feeling cut off from the people I used to brainstorm with. Where can I go for help—maybe even some guidance as I work to maximize my effectiveness as a manager?

Answer: Lots of new managers experience these issues because so many people think that they should be able to do it all. Asking for help isn't a sign of weakness! It's not easy to manage people, so don't hesitate to look for guidance when you need it. So many managers try to do everything themselves because they think they need to know everything and don't want anyone to suspect they don't know it all. This is a huge mistake, and it is how many managers derail careers. You're ahead of the game to have recognized that you can't do it all yourself.

Consider asking if your organization would provide you with a coach who could help you as you navigate your new role. However, if that's not possible, look for mentors either inside or outside your organizations. A mentor can be extremely helpful as you seek to lead your team successfully. Be sure to select mentors who are knowledgeable and trustworthy.

You also may want to consider starting meetup sessions with other managers in your organization. Even the experienced ones will want or need help from time to time. Set a time to meet and come up with some ground rules including nothing that's said leaves the room to ensure you can be open and honest with each other. I'll bet that each manager has knowledge, a skill, or expertise that others would like to hear about and use when needed. Take advantage of those free resources.

Don't overlook your peers outside your organization. They can be real assets to you. There are often informal networking groups in which members share issues and brainstorm ideas. These can be extremely helpful, as members are likely going through similar issues and experiencing the same challenges. Of course, having rules like confidentiality is the key to success!

As you seek to improve your managerial abilities, take advantage of the vast number of webinars, podcasts, books, and articles available that tackle management issues. There are countless resources to help you gain confidence in your abilities. Check out TED Talks and YouTube videos for great ideas you can use and share with others.

I highly recommend that you become a lifelong learner. Managing is challenging, and no one has a lock on how to do it all. Every manager struggles from time to time. Constantly ask questions, read, study, and try new ideas so that you build your strength as a manager. Your people, your peers, and your senior management team will appreciate it, and you will be a better manager!

Question: I received a piece of advice that I don't understand. A colleague suggested that, because I'm a new manager, I should assemble a personal board of advisors. Any idea what she meant?

Answer: Your colleague gave you some good advice, but she could have elaborated on the subject. All managers should surround themselves with trusted advisors from whom they can solicit honest advice and feedback.

Often, this starts with members of your team. As a new manager, you can be disadvantaged because you didn't hire your team members. Nevertheless, as you get to know them, you will understand their strengths and learn who the experts in their fields are. As you grow your own team and hire people who report to you, remember you want strong, competent subordinates rather than enablers (people who will scramble to make you look good despite any misgivings they may have).

As you seek out advisors, and they should include colleagues and peers in the organization in addition to your immediate team, look for people who will not shy away from telling you:

- **The truth (rather than what they think you want to hear).** This can be a particular pitfall among individuals who report to you, so choose carefully and let your expectations be known.
- **When they think you are wrong, even if you don't ask.** You don't want to hear after the fact—after you've taken an action—that others saw a potential problem. You want to hear early when people think you're making or about to make a mistake.
- **Where your blind spots are.** We're all influenced by past experiences and often don't want to admit our weakness to ourselves. All the more reason to have people who aren't afraid to point these out to us in a respectful manner.

In choosing advisors, you want people who are not afraid to challenge your ideas, argue and debate about them with you, and even slow you down in order to make you rethink some things. Solicit ideas from individuals with diverse points of views. Bring them together and let them debate. Pay attention to what they are saying and recognize when they know more about a certain topic than you do. It's particularly important to seek input from those people on a regular basis.

As you build your team of trusted advisors, solicit feedback. Ask what they see as your strengths and opportunities to develop as a manager and what they think you can do better. Query your staff about how they feel about working with you. Ask your colleagues if they've heard any comments from your staff. Embrace the feedback and don't be defensive if you don't agree!

Resist the temptation to just be with people with whom you're familiar, such as former colleagues from other organizations. Instead, surround yourself with people who will push you out of your comfort zone. This will help you to learn and grow within the organization and within your particular field.

Cultivate your external network as well. Build a strong external network that includes colleagues working in other organizations, consultants, and service providers. This will keep you up-to-date on the latest practices in your profession and industry and build your credibility.

Question: I'm a new manager and have been told I have to prepare a budget for my department. This is new to me, and I don't know where to start. Should I just take last year's budget and increase everything by a certain percent?

Answer: Preparing a budget can be daunting, even for experienced managers, so it's good to get some guidance. There are several budgeting methods that organizations may use, and they may vary by industry, so you should check with your finance department before proceeding. Two commonly used methods are incremental budgeting and zero-based budgeting.

If *incremental budgeting* is used, the budget from the prior year or the department's actual performance forms the basis and incremental amounts are added for the new budget period. Everything is based upon the previous period and simply increased by a set percentage, just as you suggested. However, this doesn't account for the realities of current and future market conditions, nor new needs or objectives for the department. Any new funds that are requested must be justified and based on department needs and objectives.

With this method, there is also the temptation for managers to fall into the use-it-or-lose-it trap, feeling compelled to use all the expenditures by the end of the period, whether they need to or not, so the following period's budget will not be reduced.

In *zero-based budgeting,* each budget cycle begins as though the budget was being prepared for the first time. The budget is prepared from scratch with all objectives and operations given a priority ranking. Then available funds are given in priority order. All expenditures are justified for each new period.

The advantage of this method is that managers are required to perform a critical, in-depth analysis of each line item. They must consider objectives, explore alternatives, and justify their requests. This analysis is very time-consuming and can be seen as a disadvantage.

Despite the method used in your organization, some common items found in a department's budget include, but are not necessarily limited to:

- Labor costs, including salaries and benefits.
- Operating costs, such as materials and supplies, office supplies, telephone, postage, travel, training, equipment rental, and contractual services.
- Capital outlay such as machinery and equipment.

If your organization uses a shared services model, you may also have cost allocations from other departments such as human resources or IT. These allocations are generally added, so you will not have to calculate them.

Your finance department, if you have one, will be able to provide you with further information on the specific method used, as well as guidance for preparing your budget for the next fiscal year. In addition to any written material they may provide, ask to meet so they can review the instructions with you and answer your questions. If you don't have someone internally to ask, there are plenty of books and tutorials available online.

Question: I've gotten through the budget process for the next fiscal year and my department's budget has been approved. Is there anything else that I need to know about financial issues?

Answer: Part of being a good manager is understanding the business of business—not just how your department functions, but how others function as well. Finance plays a big role in any organization, and every manager must develop some degree of financial literacy.

There are three important financial statements that you should understand. What these statements are called may vary in for-profit and not-for-profit organizations, but the concepts are the same. They include the:

- **Balance sheet,** which shows what the organization owns (its assets) and what it owes (its liabilities on a particular date). Assets can be physical or tangible (buildings, equipment, or inventory) or intangible (trademarks or patents). Liabilities can include rent, loans, payroll, or taxes. The difference between assets and liabilities represents what the organization is worth. Hopefully it's a positive number.

- **Income statement,** which shows how much money the organization made (revenue) and how much it spent (expenses) over a period of time, such as a year. Expenses include cash expenses made (such as rent or payroll) as well as non-cash expenses (such as depreciation of assets). Depreciation is a non-cash expense that represents the amount the value of an asset has decreased over its presumed useful life. The difference between revenue and expenses is the net earnings (profit) or loss for the period.

- **Cash flow statement,** which shows how much cash the organization has on hand. It reflects the changes in cash affected by operating activities or investments, for example. It is similar to a bank statement, which shows the amount of cash available at the beginning of a period, how much cash was deposited, how much was spent, and how much is left at the end of the period.

Understanding these basic financial statements is important for any manager. Seek out someone in your organization—a financial point person—who can help you interpret financial information for your organization. Ask them to define terms that you may not understand. Share what you learn with your department members so they can appreciate the financial health of the organization. Consider starting staff meetings with a financial update; review business and financial results. Sharing this information will help them to understand the impact that their work has on the overall organization's success.

Question: My organization has a strategic plan to which all departments must conform, but I'm not sure where mine fits. Can you give me some insights?

Answer: Strategic planning is a process that assists an organization in deciding what it wants to achieve during a certain defined period of time. Strategic plans, which are the written documentation that result from the planning process, enable organizations to make cross-functional decisions in order to remain competitive, prosper, and grow. A strategic plan helps management and employees stay focused. It allows organizations to allocate resources (financial, intellectual, and human capital, for example), identify opportunities and threats (new products, technologies, or competitors, for example), be proactive in addressing opportunities and threats, and approach problem-solving in an integrated manner. Developing these plans takes time, which is why all departments need to be aligned.

Many organizations expect that each department will also develop its own strategic plan. If this is the case, it is imperative that department plans align with the organization's plan. Some questions to consider as you embark on this process are:

- What are the organization's plans for growth, if any?
- How does your department's work support those plans?
- Are there significant changes in your industry, among your competitors, or with technology?
- How have these changes affected your department?
- How accurate have your department's past budgets and projections been? What can be done to improve their accuracy?

As a manager, it's important that you learn and understand as much as possible about your organization and its business and/or strategic plan. Here are some practical tips and strategies:

- Recognize where your department fits into the big picture. If you're a support or staff department such as accounting, human resources, or IT, represent your team as service providers for the entire organization. If your department provides core products or services, then understand if there will be new offerings, a consolidation of offerings, or introduction of new technologies that will affect the work of your team.
- Learn as much as you can about your industry. Network inside and outside the organization. Serve on internal task forces outside the scope of your traditional duties. Don't forget to encourage your team to do the same.
- If you're a support department, position yourself as an internal consultant based on your expertise. If you provide core services, then assume a decision-making stance and be prepared to provide options and solutions to senior management.
- Always use facts and objective data to support your suggestions and options. Information is valuable and will allow you to leverage your knowledge and authority.
- Build partnerships across the organization. Doing so will broaden your perspective, allowing you to more accurately represent the needs of the entire organization and make strategic and appropriate recommendations.

Remember that strategic plans aren't static. The external environment changes quickly and often, and the leaders in your organization may be making continuous adjustments. It's important that you maintain awareness of changes in your functional area so that you and your team can also adjust.

Question: I know that metrics are important in business today and a great deal of focus is placed on data analysis. I need to understand some of the basics of measurement and measurement techniques. Can you help?

Answer: You are absolutely correct. Understanding data, how it's analyzed, and how it's used to measure effectiveness and efficiency in organizations is critical. In looking at measurement techniques, organizations are often looking at financial measures as well as performance measures.

There are some basic financial measures you need to know. They are:

- **Return on investment, or ROI,** which is a calculation that compares the money earned or lost on an investment to the amount of money that was invested. In calculating ROI, the value of the benefits received is divided by the operation costs expended to produce the benefits.
- **Cost-benefit analysis,** which is a ratio of the value of the projected benefits to the costs. It allows management to determine the financial impact a particular activity or program will have on the organization's profitability. The higher the cost benefit, the more valuable the activity or program. This analysis is often used in deciding whether to proceed with a new product or program.
- **Break-even analysis,** which is a simple form of cost-benefit analysis that allows management to determine the point at which total revenue is equal to the total cost. It helps determine the minimum output that must be exceeded for a product or program to be profitable.

These financial measures are used along with examining an organization's income statement and balance sheet (which are discussed in an earlier question in this chapter), to determine the organization's overall financial health. Beyond financial measures, organizations want to measure their performance around key objectives or business processes (sales, marketing, human resources, customer relations, or production, for example). Performance is measured against goals that have been set—organization-wide goals or department-wide goals.

A number of tools and methodologies have emerged that help organizations measure performance.

- **Scorecards or balanced scorecards** measure and compare performance against projections and goals. They evaluate success or failure based on key performance indicators (KPIs), measurable values that evaluate if objectives and targets are being reached. Organizations can use them to evaluate if they are on track in meeting their goals, assess trends and patterns, and utilize resources more wisely.
- **Dashboards** are information-management tools that track KPIs, metrics, and other data relevant to the entire organization or a specific department or process. They visually display complex data in a simple manner to provide at-a-glance views. Based on the concept of a car's dashboard, which contain gauges and indicators to tell you how the vehicle is performing, dashboards can combine a number of different reports including scorecards that can be easily seen and read. Reports are typically one page.

Key performance indicators will vary by organization and industry, but often include customer metrics (e.g., customer retention and satisfaction), process metrics (e.g., customer support tickets or percentage of product defects), and people metrics (e.g., employee turnover rate or employee satisfaction), in addition to financial metrics.

You should become familiar with the tools and performance indicators that your current organization uses and become comfortable using them for your department. Talk with your manager about what's important to her and share this with your staff. Let your staff know how you and the department is being measured so you can all share in the success!

Question: I know one of my responsibilities is to manage my organization's resources, but I am not quite sure if I understand them all. Can you help me?

Answer: Yes, you're absolutely right that it is critical to any organization's success that we effectively manage resources to optimize performance. Let's look at them in some detail:

- **Human Resources:** Without the right people with the right skills in the right jobs, your organization will not succeed. It's just that simple! It is vital to your success to attract, hire, engage, and retain the best possible talent available. This requires a well-crafted workforce plan to ensure you hire people with the skills and abilities you need now and going forward. Once you hire them, you have to bring them on board in a way that they absorb your organizational culture and become productive as quickly as possible. Then, it is important to develop their skills and abilities and give them frequent feedback on their performance so that they know what they're doing well and where improvement is needed.

- **Time Resources:** Time is an infinite resource and, if not properly managed, it can have a negative impact on both the organization and the employees' productivity. One of your roles as a manager is to help your employees manage their time effectively. You can help by providing tools for effective time management, which might include setting milestones for accomplishing tasks, providing software for project management, or training on effective time-management skills.

- **Financial Resources:** No organization can succeed without effectively managing its financial resources and one of the most effective ways of accomplishing this is by a well-crafted budgeting process in which you and other managers project what financial resources you will require to meet your organization's strategic objectives. It's not enough, however, to budget—there has to be an accounting as to how each department or function is doing relative to the budget. If there are variances, decisions must be made on how to resolve the difference between budgets and actual costs. You play a vital role in monitoring how your department uses the financial resources you're provided.

- **Intellectual Property Resources:** Most likely, your organization has proprietary assets, including information or products that must be protected. You and your employees must carefully follow procedures to keep the intellectual property safe.

- **External Resources:** There is also the possibility you will be called upon to manage external resources. For example, if your organization uses a third party to source potential new employees, you may need to interact with them to provide information, follow up on the status of work, or critique their performance. The key to managing outside vendors is to set clear expectations as to what you want them to do, and when, and hold them accountable—just as you would your internal partners and employees. A great way to find an outside resource is to ask your professional network for recommendations, interview each possible organization, and check references before contracting. Be sure to follow any procurement guidelines that may be in place in your organization.

Always treat the organization's resources as if they were your own. Effectively managing resources, be they internal or external, is a key responsibility for any successful manager.

Question: How should I go about planning for my people needs for next year and beyond? I've heard there's something called "workforce planning" but I don't know where to start.

Answer: Workforce planning is the process organizations use to analyze its current workforce and its potential needs for new skills. It is usually based on the organization's strategic plan. Among the many issues considered in a workforce plan are:

- Is the organization going to grow and if so, what skills are needed and where will the jobs be located?
- Is the organization going to need to downsize or outsource positions? If so, can any of the affected employees be trained to take on new responsibilities?

Workforce planning focuses on developing information that can help you make good decisions for both the short and long term with the realization that plans, no matter how well thought out, may need to be revised to meet the changing business climate. Therefore, plans need to be evaluated often and revised as needed.

Here's how to craft a workforce plan:

1. Conduct a current workforce analysis:
   - List current employees and their skills/abilities/ strengths.
   - Look at who might retire or leave the organization and what gaps that creates.
   - Review historic turnover (attrition) data.
   - Are there any poor performers who need to be retrained or be terminated?
   - How will the current workforce impact (positively or negatively) achieving stated goals and objectives as outlined in your strategic plan?
2. Determine what knowledge/skills and abilities will be required to achieve business objectives for the next year based on:
   - Mission and vision.
   - Budget and economic forecasts.
   - Competitive factors in your line of business.
   - Labor force trends.
   - Pending or existing government regulations.
   - Innovations in technology.
   - Outsourcing options.
   - Strategic partner option.
   - Potential mergers and/or acquisitions.
   - New products.
   - Expanding to new locations.
3. Do a gap analysis to determine the gaps that exist between what you have and what you need. Answer these questions:

- Can current employees be trained to take on new responsibilities? If not, how will you deal with them (transfer to other departments, demote, terminate)?
- Do you need to hire from the outside?
- If you need to hire, when does new staff need to be on board and trained?
- Is your organization doing what it needs to do to retain key employees?
- Is the organizational structure what it should be to accomplish the goals and objectives?

You now have a plan that should tell you when and how you need to add people or skills to meet your organization's strategic objectives.

4. Implement the workforce plan. No plan is ever successful without an implementation phase to translate the actions into a workable schedule that includes well-defined objectives, specific and measurable workforce goals, and timetables and milestones. Although workforce planning isn't a simple process, the results will be very important as you plan ahead. It's worth it!

Question: I want to bring the absolute best people into my department but lately, our job offers aren't being accepted and we either have to start the recruiting process all over or offer the job to a less-qualified candidate. How do I do better at getting applicants to accept job offers?

Answer: Take a hard look at your hiring process and answer these questions:

- **Are you offering competitive salaries and benefits?**
  Participate in salary surveys in your market and check out salary and benefits information available online and then make changes, if needed. You at least want to be competitive—and, if possible, better than your competition.

- **Is your hiring process easy to navigate?** Your application and interview process need to be as candidate friendly as possible. Don't make people come back for interviews. Put a day of interviewing together and be sure that everyone who interviews or assists the candidate is trained in how to interview.
- **Do you listen carefully to what the candidate wants?** Applicants usually share what's important to them in the interview process. If career progression is their hot button, stress your commitment to professional development (if that's true) when you make the offer. Another candidate may share that having a mentor is what's critical to them, so when you make the offer tell them who their mentor will be.
- **Do you know your organization's reputation?** If there is negative press out there about the organization, deal with it as quickly as possible and head it off by being honest with your candidate. Let them know that you're aware there are some issues but that concrete steps are being taken to improve the culture or resolve the issues. Transparency and honesty are impressive and may be the deciding factor for your number-one choice.
- **How are you making job offers?** Have the hiring manager call the candidate and make a verbal offer. This sends the message that you really want them and are excited about having them work with you. HR should then send a written offer that is exactly what the verbal offer said but that includes additional details to help the candidate make an informed decision (benefit details, onboarding dates and times, I-9 requirements, etc.).
- **Do you encourage candidates to call with questions and/or to negotiate?** Be prepared and know where you have flexibility. This may be the key to getting a potential superstar so be as flexible as possible.

A best practice is to constantly evaluate your hiring process. Odds are you will learn something that will improve your process. You also may want to think about keeping in touch with the great candidates that turn you down. You never know what happens to them after they reject your offer; they may reconsider.

Question: The leadership in my organization really is anxious to get on a "best place to work list," either nationally or locally. Our major competitor was recently selected for this honor, so we need to keep up! I totally get why this is important, but I don't have a clue where to start. Any ideas?

Answer: Before you do anything else, think about whether or not your organization is really a good place to work, because if you're not ready, it is pointless to go through the application process. Being recognized as a great place to work is a noble goal for any organization but be prepared—it is not an easy or quick process to make this happen.

I'd start by researching what the best places to work do for their employees. Organizations that frequently are named best places to work are known for:

- Constantly reinforcing their mission so that everyone knows they are working for more than just a paycheck.
- Paying fairly and as competitively as possible so that employees are paid a living wage and providing the best benefits the organization can afford.
- Making the work environment as comfortable, safe, and appealing as possible. No matter what the office configuration is, having plenty of spaces for private conversations and places where people can go to de-stress during the work day is important. Some organizations have game tables in break rooms or even a nap room for some quiet time. "Huddle" spaces (places where people can gather in colorful surroundings to encourage creativity) are very popular.

- Clearly outlining expectations for each and every employee and measuring performance against those expectations.
- Giving frequent feedback—constructive *and* positive. Don't wait for the annual review; give feedback often. Many organizations are moving toward having frequent performance conversations at the end of a project or at least quarterly as opposed to an annual review.
- Recognizing and rewarding great employees for their ideas and contributions but doing it in a way that honors the employee—and remembering that some people don't want to be praised in public.
- Holding everyone accountable for treating others with respect.
- Providing opportunities for employees to develop their skills through mentoring, webinars, podcasts, workshops, books—whatever works for that person.
- Making their employees proud by being visible in their community.

The overall goal is to have a workforce that is committed to the work you do. To do that, you need everyone in the organization pulling in the same direction. Then, and only then, you can start applying for recognition as a great place to work.

When you're ready to apply, consider starting with local lists. For example, does your city do an annual list of great employers in your area? Start there and work up to the national or international lists when you've had some experience with what's required to be considered.

Question: I know my organization has an Employee Assistance Program, but I don't know much about it. Other than helping with personal problems, does it provide any other services or value?

Answer: Employee Assistance Programs (EAPs) are continuing to grow in importance as workplace and societal issues grow more complex and managers must deal with more difficult challenges. A good EAP provider that interfaces with management and the organization offers much to their clients and is a tremendous resource for every executive, manager, and employee.

You are probably most familiar with the EAP's role in assisting troubled employees with personal problems that are affecting their lives, especially when those problems are affecting their work life. They can also explain health benefits and be a resource for employees taking leave for family medical issues, workers' compensation, or short-term and long-term disability. Many have staff that can assist employees at all levels expand their development opportunities.

For the organization, the EAP can serve as a resource for systemic issues facing the organization. Their counselors are often trained in change management and a systems approach to organizational problem-solving. They also have expertise in behavioral health and the impact of mental health issues in the workplace. Therefore, they can identify potential behavioral risks associated with conflict, work practices, and poor supervision. Another way that an EAP can support the organization is offering grief counseling and response to critical incidents. For example, should an employee die, regardless of the nature of the death, EAP counselors can be available for grief counseling for the rest of the team. They can also provide support if a tragic situation occurs in the workplace or the community.

What can an EAP do for you, as the manager? It can help you to recognize and intervene with workplace performance and behavior problems (for example, helping you spot signs and symptoms of behavior that could potentially lead to workplace violence). This kind of proactive involvement increases the early identification of employees' behavioral health problems and decreases the cost of these problems for the organization. It also takes stress off managers who don't have the same knowledge or training that the professionals have.

The following are some ways an EAP can provide value and assistance to you in your job as a manager:

- Provide consultation to help you strategize and develop plans for dealing with employees with job performance problems.

- Coach you through difficult conversations with employees with job performance problems.
- Provide training for all managers regarding use of the EAP as a management tool.
- Provide training for managers regarding signs and symptoms of drug abuse or potential workplace violence.
- Provide crisis management and consultation services.
- Assist in preventing workplace violence.
- Identify potential behavioral risks associated with conflict or work practices.

An EAP is a corporate risk-management tool available to all levels of the organization. The strength of an EAP is assisting both the system and individual and its ability to be part of the strategy to maximize performance and potential. You should check with your internal resources, likely your human resources support, to find out more information about your organization's EAP provider.

Question: A number of outside firms provide services and support to my organization. Part of my new responsibility is to oversee these third-party contractors. What should I be looking for when I review and evaluate them?

Answer: This can be a daunting responsibility, especially if you were not involved in selecting these services. The best place to start is to get a copy of the contract your organization signed with them and review it. Any contract or service level agreement will detail the specific services that have been agreed upon. Other items that could be contained in the contract that will be helpful are any management reports that the contractor is required to furnish to you detailing the services provided during a specific period (monthly, quarterly, or annually). Often these will highlight significant events.

Contracts can also contain provisions for the contractor's internal quality assurance—those actions they will take in the event that errors or omissions occur. There may also be information about the contractor's internal tracking, analysis, and reporting systems. It should also specify the account management team and the experience level of the staff working on your account. You should also have an understanding of any measurements that are being used to evaluate the quality and effectiveness of the services being provided. Your legal and/or procurement support can help you with these issues.

You'll want to review any reports that have been received, preferably for the past twelve months, to get a sense of how they've been performing. In addition, talk to your internal staff and get their feedback.

Finally, you'll want to meet with the contractor's account manager and establish a relationship with him or her. Get their perspective about how things are going.

Whenever you have oversight for a third-party contractor, there is always the question of when you should consider new vendors. Don't assume that because contractor oversight is now your responsibility, it's an opportunity to change or to bring in someone with whom you've worked before. If this contractor is performing according to the terms of the agreement, making a change may not be wise. There are also contractual issues that need to be considered.

Here are some considerations about changing vendors:

- Has the current vendor's business model changed and their focus is moving away from the services they have been providing?
- Are there a significant number of new vendors in the marketplace that may have more robust solutions?
- Is your current vendor not performing? If that's the case, what are the contract provisions for non-performance? Have you met all those provisions, such as notifying the account manager and providing an opportunity to fix the problem? Make sure you understand your organization's obligations. Be sure that you work with your legal team if you need to terminate a contract for this reason.
- Is the current contract about to expire? Most contracts have a set period. There may be provisions for add-on years or add-on services, or provisions for renewal. Check with procurement and legal. Contract expiration

can be an optimal time to look at the market, even if your current vendor is providing good service.

Question: I want to develop into more of a strategic thinker but need some help on how to get started. Can you give me some advice?

Answer: Congratulations on your desire to up your game by thinking more strategically. Strategic thinking ability is more and more in demand as you advance in your career, so getting started early is a key.

Many people confuse strategic thinking with strategic planning. *Strategic thinking* is defined as a process in which people think about, assess, view, and create the future for themselves and others. Strategic thinking can be used to make both business and personal decisions, so it is a valuable skill to have—both as a manager and as a human being. *Strategic planning* is a business activity that is used to set priorities, focus organizational energy and resources, strengthen operations, and allocate human capital to ensure the organization is heading toward an agreed-upon goal. Strategic thinking is certainly a valuable skill when doing strategic planning, but these are two very different processes.

Strategic thinkers imagine what could be; they don't just look at what already exists in an organization. They bring a fresh approach to potential new products, services, and markets. Strategic thinking is a forward-facing process and a major driver to any organization's success.

If you want to be a strategic thinker, you need to open your mind to possibilities. This is difficult for many managers, as we're trained to deal with what's real (not what's imagined). Open your mind to looking for new solutions to old problems.

A great way to start developing your strategic thinking skills is to ask questions such as:

- What is working and what's not working now?
- How does our best work get done?
- Are we sure what our clients, customers, or members really think about our work?
- What values do we display as a team or organization?

- How many of our employees know our mission, vision, and/or values?
- How many of our employees know where their work fits into our mission?

It's almost impossible to think strategically if you're constantly busy, so set aside time to research and dream. Give your employees permission to do the same, and reward your people for great ideas that can come from strategic thinking. When you find an employee who is especially good at strategic thinking, consider asking that person to mentor others.

So many organizations and managers get stuck doing things the same way they've always done them. The death of strategic thinking is when someone makes a suggestion to change a process and someone says, "We tried that in 2005 and it didn't work then, so why would we think it will work now?" Well, there are lots of reasons why, even if it didn't work then, it has the chance of working now—so give it a try! Don't be a naysayer.

Strategic-thinking ability is a valued skill in any size organization and can differentiate you from your peers, so get started today and build your skills!

Question: I've just been asked to lead a task force that will be comprised of representatives from across the organization. I want to approach this as a project manager would. What are the key issues in project management for which I should prepare?

Answer: You are certainly on the right track. A project is a series of tasks and activities, which is exactly what your task force will be undertaking. Although projects and task forces vary in size and scope, there are common characteristics.

- **Stated goals and objectives**: what you are tasked to do or the organizational need that must be fulfilled and how you are going to achieve the goal(s).
- **Schedule:** the allotted time frame in which to complete the project.

- **Resources:** the people, equipment, time, and money budgeted for the project.

Once all of these are in place, the next step is to staff the project, starting with the project manager. Because you will be in that role, you will have overall control and responsibility for the project and the work of your task force members. You will be:

- The liaison between the task force and the rest of the organization.
- The spokesperson responsible for gathering and disseminating information.
- The decision-maker who allocates resources, encourages progress, and negotiates differences.

As the project manager, you may be responsible for selecting other members of the team or task force. Be sure that you understand the special knowledge, skills, and expertise that need to be represented on the team in making these selections.

Once the team is in place, you'll move to the next phases of the project, namely:

- **Planning, Scheduling, Monitoring, and Control:** This is where most of the work of the project is accomplished, and you'll be responsible for monitoring the quality of the work, the quantity or progress against the time frame set for the project, and the use of resources that have been allocated to the project. You goal, obviously, is to deliver the finished project on time and on budget. You must also be able to anticipate any obstacles that could hinder the project's successful completion and be able to take immediate action to remove them.

  There are several tools that help with project planning. The first is a Gantt chart or horizontal bar chart, which graphically displays activities of a project in sequential order and plots them against time. Another tool is a PERT (program evaluation review technique) chart, which details project milestones and the sequence in which tasks need to be completed.

- **Evaluation:** Depending on the size and scope of the project, evaluation can take place at various phases or predetermined times (e.g., every month). Either way, a final evaluation will need to take place once the project is completed.
- **Completion:** This is where everyone gets to take a step back and enjoy the culmination—the successful launch of the project. The completion should be documented in a report that details the project's accomplishments and gaps, lessons learned for future, similar projects, and, if necessary, what next steps are needed.

Be sure you communicate throughout the course of the project. In fact, you should build communication updates into the project plan. Provide updates on the project's progress and identify successes and milestones. Keeping the leadership, external and internal stakeholders, and your task force team members apprised of the progress will enhance the project's success.

Closing Thoughts

You'll have lots of questions as you develop your managerial skills over time. Surround yourself with trusted advisors and mentors, and take every opportunity to learn new skills. Take advantage of all that's available on line or offered by your organization to add to your skill base. You may find the next section of this book to be particularly helpful as you build your skills.

Developing Your Management Skills

THERE IS ALWAYS something new to learn in your work to become the best manager possible. Any manager, whether new or experienced, needs to constantly be building and fine-tuning their skills. This section provides suggestions and best practices for doing just that. You should never stop learning new skills and putting them into practice!

Question: I think my organization wastes a huge amount of time in meetings and I'd like to see us get better at making them as efficient as possible. What can we do?

Answer: Ask any manager (or any employee, for that matter) if they think their organization has too many meetings and the answer will be *yes!* You're on the right track to see what can be done to maximize the time spent in meetings because they're a fact of life in today's collaborative workplaces. The trick is to learn how to manage them so they don't waste your team's time and energy. Here are some ideas for making meetings more efficient and more productive:

- Develop ground rules, such as "We start and end meetings on time," "Everyone has an equal voice in meetings," and "One person speaks at a time." Post the ground rules in every conference room, and until they become part of your culture, start each meeting by reviewing your ground rules.

- Before you schedule a meeting, consider whether the information could be shared via email or by a quick phone call.
- Invite the right people to your meeting. If a colleague isn't directly involved in the decision to be made or doesn't have information that no one else has, consider not including him, but let him know why. Odds are he will be thrilled to have the time available for other work.
- Always have an agenda and assign times to each topic. Send the agenda out ahead of time so people can come prepared. Have a timekeeper to help the facilitator stay on schedule. The agenda should start with the most important topic. This should help get people there on time.
- If there are action items from the last meeting be sure they are on the agenda and the people responsible are ready to update their progress.
- If you, as the leader of the meeting, want to actively participate in it, consider asking someone else to be the facilitator. It is difficult to participate and facilitate.
- Assign a note-taker to write and share the minutes within an agreed-upon time.
- The facilitator should encourage everyone to participate in the discussions. If the right people are invited and the agenda shared in advance, everyone should be ready to participate. Remember that introverts don't tend to speak up unless asked or unless they've had time to process the information being shared. Don't overlook them—they may have the solution you've been looking for.
- Try some new meeting formats. Stand-up meetings tend to be productive and quick. They don't work if you have a lot of topics to discuss but can be very effective when there is one decision to be made. Consider a "walking

meeting." Let people know ahead of time that the meeting will be held on a walk around your building or in your neighborhood, and remind them to dress appropriately for the weather. People can be more creative when they are walking and moving rather than just sitting. The ideal number of participants is two to four, so that you listen to each other's ideas.

We know that with a few changes like these, your organization can maximize the time spent in meetings so give it a try.

Question: We are experiencing some major changes due to economic pressures. What should we be doing to keep our employees informed?

Answer: The interesting thing about change is that we each choose how to approach it.

- **Innovators/change agents embrace change as an opportunity.** They seek answers to questions, look for ways to move change forward, and easily adapt.
- **Pragmatics take a wait-and-see approach.** They do whatever is possible to stay out of sight and out of harm's way, keeping quiet and waiting to see who wins. Pragmatics thus withhold their sponsorship and energy.
- **Skeptics/traditionalists resist change, actively or passively.** They significantly affect the organization's ability to move forward and can negatively impact morale.

Helping employees understand their response toward change helps frame their actions. Though change is often uncomfortable, it can also bring a whole new energy level to the organization. As soon as everyone gets on board with the change, things can happen that move the group/team/department forward. The challenge is getting through the change and conflicts to get to the other side!

When people are open to the possibilities that the change may bring, they share some of the responsibility for making it successful. However, if people are not sure what is happening, and they do not feel responsible for the outcome, they will actively or passively resist the change. Everyone needs to understand how the change will affect them. They need to know where they fit. For example:

- What are the business drivers?
- What are the job expectations? Have they changed?
- How have roles and responsibilities changed?

Leaders and managers can support employees during periods of change by:

- Providing them with honest feedback.
- Helping them find answers to their questions.
- Being clear in communicating expectations.
- Encouraging them to connect, inquire, and perform—in other words, to take positive action.
- Actively listening to what's being said.
- Understanding the root causes of resistance.

During periods of change, managers must be on the lookout for conflicts to ensure that changes positively drive the results the organization is seeking. The steps you take to mitigate the effects of that change will determine the types of conflicts that occur, and whether conflict and change is a constructive or destructive force for your organization.

Question: I just found out that I need to make a formal presentation to our leadership. This is a great opportunity for me to gain visibility in the organization and maybe get a promotion. Can you give me some pointers so that I hit it out of the park?

Answer: Most people start putting their slides together before taking the time to think about their objective. Is the presentation to inform or is it a call to action? When you're clear on the objective, lay out your three to four key points. Keep it simple so that your audience can easily grasp your message.

There's an old adage about presentations that still holds true today: *Tell them what you're going to tell them. Tell them. Then tell them what you told them.* With this audience, don't even think of opening with a joke—get right to the point of your presentation. State it clearly at the beginning and say it again near the middle and again at the end. A strong opening will make a big impression on the audience.

Here's the hard part—you want to appear calm and in control as you start your presentation and throughout. This is why you need to know your material well and rehearse it as often as needed so that you can deliver it comfortably. Only you know how much time you need to practice, but be sure you're ready in plenty of time!

Before your presentation, spend some time in the room where the meeting will take place to get a sense of where people will be sitting and the best spot for you to stand. Practice with the technology you will be using so that when you stand up to speak, you can move right into your presentation.

A day or so before you will be speaking, do a dry run, if possible, to be sure your slides can be read from anywhere in the room. If you will be using notes, number the pages so that if you drop them as you stand up to speak, you can quickly put them in order.

You can't rehearse too much. You want to be confident with your material so your audience will have confidence in you. Consider asking a trusted colleague to sit in on your rehearsal to give you feedback and to tell you where you need more data or a better explanation. This step can also help you anticipate the questions you'll get at the end of your presentation.

If you start with a clear objective, carefully prepare your material, and rehearse your presentation so that you can be as comfortable possible, you'll be just fine. Trust me: It gets easier every time you make a presentation.

Question: I understand that storytelling is an excellent way to share information. Is that true, and if so, can you give me some insights and advice on how I can be a good storyteller?

Answer: Your instincts are right. Narrative contributes to the role of managing and telling a story is an excellent tool because people are more likely to recall something when they've heard it told within a story. Stories capture people's attention and imagination. They are a great way to convey a message, share an experience, and inspire your team. Stories align people and make them more effective in sharing information.

As you craft your stories, keep these attributes of a story in mind:

- Endurance. Are there lessons that will remain with the audience?
- Salience. Is the story funny, clever, and moving?
- Sensible. Does it explain something, show a cause and effect, for example?
- Relevant. Is it clear, distinct, consistent and focused?

How do you construct a good story? Make sure it has a beginning, middle, and end.

- Where you've come from, your "once upon a time" or a "long time ago in a galaxy far, far away."
- Where you are now? What obstacles are you trying to overcome? This is where the story gains tension and raises the stakes. This is where people begin to pay attention in a way they weren't before.
- Where you are heading (your ending)? In constructing your story, you should figure out where you want to be first.

Consider your objective as you craft your story. If you want to:

- Spark action, then you need a story that illustrates a similar past event, such as a similar change successfully implemented before.
- Communicate who you are, then your story should reveal some strength or vulnerability of your past.
- Foster collaboration, then your story must recount a situation the audience has experienced to prompt them to share their experiences.
- Share knowledge, then you may want your story to focus on past mistakes then show how they were corrected.

As you develop your story, be mindful of the following:

- Know your audience.
- Make sure the audience wants to hear your story. Connect your story to the key message that you want to convey.

- Use context. Plot, setting, sounds—all of the things particular to the set—help to explain how you've gotten to where you and/or your team are now.
- The positive side of your story should be the major theme. You may be sharing a situation in which you were vulnerable in the past, but the lesson you learned is your positive outcome.
- Humor brightens your story and having a touch of emotion adds some spice, but don't overdo it!
- Understand the essence of your story—the most economical way of telling it. This is your trailer, your summary, your happily ever after!
- Be able to shorten or lengthen your story to fit the situation.

In telling stories, you'll want to get people's attention first, then provide them with some facts. Make your points and then move on. Don't belabor the facts or ramble. Keep the story brief and to the point, but tell it with passion. When you become known as a great storyteller, people will want to be in your meetings and presentations. They'll seek you out as a leader!

Question: I really don't want to give up my favorite tasks and projects, but I know I need to delegate to help my staff learn and grow and so I can have more time to do my managerial duties. Any advice how I can do this without looking as if I am putting my work off on others?

Answer: Many people believe delegation is the number-one management skill, so not being a good delegator can derail your management career, and you certainly don't want that to happen!

It is impossible for you, now that you're responsible for the work of others, to not delegate—not just because it is the right thing to do for your staff, but because there are only so many hours in the day. You can't manage and do all the things you used to do before your promotion.

It's amazing how many managers don't delegate because they think it is quicker to do the task themselves. At first, that may be true, but if you take the time to teach your staff member how to do it, you probably only have to do that once and your employee may even be better at it than you were. They may be able to accomplish the task quicker or add something to it that never occurred to you and improve its outcome. And, you now have more time to do something else!

Before you delegate a task, think carefully about which of your staff members is right for the job. Who has the required skill set? This requires you to know the strengths and weaknesses of all your staff members. When you have the right person, here are the important steps to take to ensure the task is successfully accomplished:

- Describe the task to the employee, and let them know when you want it completed and what you want the result of their work on the task to be. Answer all their questions so that there is clarity on both sides. It is a good idea to set times for you to check in on how they're doing, but be sure you are clear that they can come to you at any time with questions while they're working on the task.
- Be clear about how you will measure success, and be sure that what you agree to is realistic and attainable. Nothing is quite so discouraging to an employee than to be asked to accomplish something that is impossible!
- As you're describing the task and the desired outcome, don't forget the context. People work better when they understand why they're being asked to do something, so don't just share the *how* but give them the *why* as well. Let them know they have your full support and that you will back them up!

When you delegate tasks, not only do you free up your time to work on more strategic tasks, you develop your employee's skills and give them greater visibility in your organization. This is what good managers do!

Question: My days are different now that I'm a manager. It seems there just is not enough time to get everything done. What should I be doing better to make the best use of my time?

Answer: Time management is certainly a challenge for everyone, not just managers. That's not to say that managers do not have more and varied demands made on them and on their time. The challenge is confronting and managing these demands.

Begin by tracking how you spend your time for several days. That will give you some insights on where you are best utilizing and wasting time. You know you need to delegate tasks, and there are good tips in the previous question to help you do so. Beyond delegation, consider the following:

- Use a to-do list. Listing all of the tasks that need to be done is a good way to keep you on track and to experience a sense of accomplishment once you cross off a task. Be specific and detailed as you write down your tasks. If you have large projects or assignments, break them down into smaller tasks. Finally, keep the list visible. Don't let it get lost on your desk.
- Prioritize the tasks so you're not spending too much time on ones that seem urgent (e.g., answering a ringing phone) and not enough time on those that are important (e.g., taking care of a client).
- Keep your workspace tidy and organized. Don't let things, like your to-do list, get misplaced on your desk. You will spend less time looking for files and important papers.
- Set a schedule or routine and stick to it as best you can. For example, use the time at the beginning or end of your day to answer emails or return and make phone calls. Take some time at the end of each day to organize your workspace so you are ready for the next day.
- Manage distractions and interruptions. Don't feel compelled to answer every email or message the moment it arrives. Not everyone needs immediate attention. When people drop by to chat without an appointment, it's okay to say you're working on something important and ask them if you can get back to them.

- Don't put things off or procrastinate. Sometimes large projects can seem daunting so it's easy to push them off until you have a day to devote to them. The problem is, that day never seems to come. If you devote a small amount of time each day to large projects and complete tasks associated with it, you will avoid feeling overwhelmed.
- Avoid taking on too much. Learn to say no. This may be the biggest challenge, especially if it's your boss asking. Offer a substitute—a one-page summary versus a multi-page report, for example. Explain why you cannot attend that meeting but offer to send someone in your place if the department needs to be represented.

Guarding your time and making the best use of it is one of the most important things you can do as a manager and a leader. You'll get so much more accomplished and people will notice!

Question: I have so many new things to do now that I'm a manager and it seems my to-do list keeps growing. How can I prioritize all these tasks?

Answer: You're not alone. Even experienced managers often struggle with prioritizing as more demands are placed on their time.

As you review your to-do list, determine which tasks are *urgent* and which are *important,* the distinction being that urgent tasks demand immediate attention regardless of consequences and important tasks will have consequences if not completed. The ringing phone may appear urgent—or at least annoying—but it could be a telemarketer, and what's the consequence if you don't answer it? The report that is due to a client is important and could result in an account being lost if it's not delivered on time. Ask yourself the following as you determine if a task is important:

- What effect, if any, will it have on other people or projects if it's not completed?
- How many people or projects will it affect?
- Are there other tasks that depend on this one being completed?
- Will it contribute value?

The important tasks obviously have to take precedent. To further prioritize them, figure out which are time sensitive and have deadlines. This should help you to pick the most important tasks so you can focus on them first. The tasks that are both important and have deadlines rise to the top of the list—and those with impending deadlines obviously need to be done first. Also, are there any tasks on the list that are overdue? If so, what are the consequences, if any? Can you get an extension on the deadline?

Speaking of time, you also want to decide how much time each task on the list will take. Flag those that can be done quickly. If you have finished something major and don't have the time or energy to tackle another important task before lunch or the end of the day, that's a good time to turn your attention to the easy, low-intensity tasks. Attending to them now will move them off of your list.

Human nature being what it is, there are always things we'd prefer to be doing rather than the things we have to be doing. To further help you prioritize your list, consider the things you:

1. Don't want to do and don't need to do.
2. Don't want to do but need to do.
3. Want to do and need to do.
4. Want to do but don't need to do.

Get rid of the ones you don't need to do—numbers one and four above. Look at tasks in categories two and three. The temptation is to jump to number three—want and need to do. However, start by tackling number two. Motivate yourself to do something you don't want to by mixing it up. For example, plug in headphones and listen to music while doing it. It will make the task more enjoyable.

Good managers work smart as well as hard. They focus their energy and time. Prioritizing your tasks can help you focus on those things that matter.

Question: I'm confused about the difference between coaching and counseling. They seem to be used interchangeably but I think there is a difference. How do I know when to counsel and when to coach my employees?

Answer: You're right: Coaching and counseling are two very different managerial processes. and it's important for managers to know when and how to use each one. Coaching and counseling are very valuable and impactful management techniques. Let's look at each.

- **Coaching:** Perhaps you have a good employee who is already performing the job well but may need encouragement and support to reach the next level. They have excellent skills in most areas but need to "up their game" in other areas of the job. For example, they have all the technical parts of the job down pat but need to work on being more politically savvy.

  Because that employee is already performing at a high level, this is the time when you "coach" to improve her performance. Coaching is a thought-provoking and creative process that inspires employee to maximize their personal and professional potential.

  Another example of when you might coach an employee is when you think they have the potential to take on new responsibilities or be promoted to a higher level job. You've noticed that they consistently perform their current job at a high level and that over time they've demonstrated that they have the required abilities for the next job. However, their professional image isn't what it needs to be in order to move to higher levels in your organization. A good manager puts on their coaching hat and diplomatically provides guidance.

- **Counseling:** Counseling is used when there is a performance or conduct issue. You've noticed that the employee is having difficulty completing tasks or has an attitude problem that's getting in the way of them succeeding. The issue has to be resolved or you may need to take further action. Your goal in a counseling situation is to help the employee improve their performance or correct their behavior so that they will continue to have a job with you and contribute at the highest level possible.

Let's say you are in a sales organization and one of your team has missed their sales target for two months in a row. You need to counsel that person to determine where the breakdown is. Do they need more training or support from you? Have they lost interest in the work and need some help to regain their passion or is it time for a change in assignment? Any of these courses of action may be needed, but you have to get in there to understand the issues and do your best to help the employee improve their performance.

A successful manager is both a coach and a counselor, and knows what each employee needs at a particular point in time. You have to be a good listener and have a genuine interest in retaining the best talent available. Good managers set clear expectations and provide frequent feedback on where employees need to improve and encourage employees to learn and grow.

Question: I have to address workplace issues with an employee whose behavior isn't meeting our organization's standards. How can I do that without it appearing punitive?

Answer: Unfortunately, sometimes employees engage in behavior that is unacceptable or disruptive to others, even if the employee is performing most or all of the duties of their job. These behaviors, such as abusive language, bickering with others, absenteeism, or tardiness, can either create barriers and prevent others from doing their work or violate established standards of conduct. Either way, you do need to take corrective action and get the employee back on the right course.

Managers are often reluctant to address these issues, so it's good that you recognize your need to do so. Don't postpone taking corrective action because it's unpleasant. The problem isn't going to go away, and you aren't helping the employee by avoiding it. Left unchecked, it will be harder to correct and both the employee and you will lose credibility among the team members. You'll risk losing the respect and cooperation of your team. Unacceptable behavior affects the bottom line. Poor quality work or tensions created among the staff will eventually translate into higher costs and lower profits. Keep in mind that good performers want to work with other good performers so if you let problem behavior slide, you risk losing a top performer!

Taking corrective action doesn't mean punishing the employee. It's part of the continuous development process. Likely your organization has a progressive or corrective discipline policy in place. These usually start with a verbal warning—which you should document—and advances into several levels of written warnings and possibly suspension before termination occurs. The purpose of a progressive system is to give the employee ample opportunity to correct the behavior. It's important that you work with your human resources and/or legal staff to ensure that you understand and are applying the policy correctly.

When you sit down with the employee, there are several actions you can take to effectively implement the corrective action:

1. Point out the difference between what the employee is presently doing and what they should be doing.
2. Describe in specific terms the negative impact the employee's behavior is having on them, others, and the organization.
3. Give the employee the opportunity to explain. There could be extenuating circumstances. However, don't get caught up in defensive excuses.
4. Get input from the employee on corrective actions that can be taken—and contribute your own ideas.
5. Explain next steps you plan to take if the situation is not corrected. This should include next steps in the disciplinary process.
6. Confirm the employee's commitment to correcting the situation by having an action plan and date for follow-up.
7. Finally, express confidence in the employee's ability to correct the situation.

Taking corrective action is not a pleasant part of a manager's job, but don't let it overwhelm you. Working to maintain the employee's self-esteem sets an example for handling a tough situation. It allows you the opportunity to take direct action to avoid losing a member of your team.

Question: I have an employee who is performing up to the standards of their position, but I think they're capable of more. I'd like to coach them in order to optimize their performance and give them the opportunity to contribute more, but I don't know where to start. Do you have any advice?

Answer: You're very insightful to recognize this opportunity. Effective managers look for both problems and opportunities that occur on the job as chances to work with their team members to build skills and develop greater strengths for the future. They are always looking for opportunities to develop people, which is important.

When you use a coaching approach, you are collaborating with employees—getting them to recognize their own potential and the opportunity to strengthen their skills. You're tapping into their inherent, self-driving motivation. The result is a more highly skilled and flexible team that brings extra resources, freeing up your time to devote to management activities.

The following is a road map or coaching approach that you can integrate into your daily management practice:

1. Identify coaching opportunities—be specific—and understand why it's important to the employee, the team, and the organization.
2. Recognize how you can use the opportunity to develop the employee's potential and how it ties to their interests and career goals. In other words, what's in it for the employee?
3. Describe the opportunity and its importance to the employee. Highlighting a specific development area, as opposed to many, focuses the employee and prevents him from feeling overwhelmed. Describing its importance shows how the employee's efforts will benefit him, the team, and the organization.
4. Get the employee's opinion. This encourages him to take the initiative to analyze his own performance, evaluate his progress, and build a sense of being more responsible for his own actions and development.

5. Seek input on specific ways the employee can enhance his performance. This shows you respect his ability to solve problems and generate ideas. The best ideas often come from those closer to the work than the manager is. You also avoid the perception of imposing your own perspective on the employee.

6. Provide feedback on the employee's ideas and add your own. The employee's ideas deserve an honest reaction from you. Use your skills to teach, guide, encourage, and reinforce. Adding your own ideas gives the employee additional options to consider and provides insight into broader management and organizational perspectives.

7. Summarize what you've discussed and plan to follow up. This reaffirms what the employee has committed to do and sets a pace for the action.

8. Close on a positive note of support. This motivates and builds confidence.

Coaching should be an ongoing effort to help your employees improve poor performance, acquire new skills, and reach their full potential. Doing so allows them to take on more responsibility and won't leave you feeling as if you are carrying as much of the weight of the department.

Question: I'm noticing a skills gap among some of my employees. There are several new employees on the team, so that explains why they are struggling. However, among tenured employees, some are struggling and others are ready for new responsibilities. What can I do to bridge these gaps?

Answer: The skills required in today's organizations are constantly changing and evolving. It's great that you want to help your employees grow and change to meet these challenges. As a manager there are a number of steps you can engage in to help your team develop or strengthen their job skills, whether it's tangible skills (technical or mechanical skills such as running machines, developing a budget, or following research procedures) or intangible but important interpersonal skills (handling conflict or dealing with customers, for example).

Using the following systematic yet simple approach is much more beneficial than taking shortcuts such as providing brief explanations—and no demonstration—or suggesting that the employee can read a manual, find the information online, and figure it out for herself. However, before you begin, determine if there are any resources that the employee needs that they may not have.

1. Define the task and its importance. This enables the employee to concentrate on what you're teaching. When they understand the task's importance, it motivates the employee to learn because they see that their efforts contribute to their success.

2. Describe for the employee what it looks like to effectively perform the task. This helps her to visualize doing the task successfully and provides a concrete goal.

3. List the steps involved in performing the task, including the sequence in which they need to take place. Breaking it down into logical steps removes confusion and familiarizes the employee with the task so it's less intimidating.

4. Demonstrate or model the task. This is the most effective learning technique. Most people learn best by watching rather than by hearing how something needs to be done. Telling leaves major questions unasked and important subtleties overlooked.

5. Ask the employee to demonstrate or perform each step so you can see what they understand and what, if anything, is confusing them. Being able to practice in a safe environment will build their confidence.

6. Provide accurate and real-time feedback so the employee knows what she's doing right and where she may need to focus on improvement.

Keep in mind that some tasks that your employees may need to learn are relatively simple and can be learned relatively quickly. For these, you should see results fairly soon. Other tasks, however, can be more complex and take more time to learn. For those, it will take longer to see results or improvement. In either case, developing skills and helping your employees change and grow to meet new and emerging requirements will build your team into top performs. It will also enhance your credibility as a manager.

Question: Our workforce is very diverse. We have employees from many different cultures and countries. Can you offer any guidance or insight for managing and interacting in this environment?

Answer: Workplaces today are indeed becoming more and more diverse creating new opportunities and challenges. As more cultural groups come together we discover that each has its own way of thinking, its own values and beliefs, and different preferences. What makes each culture unique from others is where their preference for certain variables fall on different cultural dimensions. These dimensions include:

- **Our view of authority:** a preference for equal status for all, including an informal relationship with management and others or a hierarchical preference that respects a chain of command and values formal relationships.
- **How we communicate:** a preference for a direct and to-the-point approach versus a more indirect approach that is subtle and implicit.
- **Whether people place emphasis on the individual** (rewards, credit, being singled out, and individual accomplishments prized) **or on the group** (shared responsibility/accountability and individual accomplishments discouraged).
- **How we solve problems:** a preference for a linear/logical approach, with a sequential ordering of thoughts, versus a lateral/intuitive approach, with a circular and meandering thought process.
- **Our approach to work:** a preference to a task focus, with an emphasis on work and information, versus a

relationship focus, with an emphasis on building relationships and getting along with others.

- **How we resolve conflict:** a preference for dealing with conflict in a direct and open manner, in which discussing differences is viewed as productive, versus a preference for avoiding conflict and smoothing over problems, in which discussing differences is viewed as disrupted and counterproductive.
- **Our approach to change:** a preference for accepting change as progress and improvement, in which innovation is valued, versus a preference for tradition, in which change is seen as disruptive and order, stability, and the status quo are valued.
- **How we view time:** a preference for strict time consciousness, in which there is a priority on promptness and deadlines and things move at a brisk pace, versus a preference for an elastic time consciousness, in which deadlines are not treated as a top priority and the pace is more relaxed.

The best place to begin is to be aware that other people's preferences and perceptions may not be the same as yours—especially if they are from a different country. That said, of course, don't try to stereotype individuals by their country of origin, for example. Diversity exists among people within a given culture. Remember, too, that culture extends beyond national groups. It includes other social groups such as the organization in which people work, or worked, and the department or team within the organization. You may encounter differences with people who look and sound like you but join from different organizations or industries.

Try not to become impatient with others if you recognize that they approach a problem or change, for example, differently than you do. It's okay to discuss these differences. You will both learn to accept them and you may even meet in the middle.

Question: I am aware that critical thinking is important, especially for a manager. How can I improve my skills in this area?

Answer: As a manager you are going to find yourself in many situations in which people will provide you with information and try to influence or persuade you to do something. You'll have to make more and varied decisions, so it's good that you want to sharpen your critical-thinking skills.

Critical thinking is the process of making inferences and judgments about the credibility of messages and information communicated to us. The information that other people communicate to us provides the basis for many of the decisions we have to make. We also must draw on our own knowledge and experience in making decisions. If we don't exercise critical thinking, the attempts of others to influence us can have unfortunate consequences.

The key to critical thinking is to examine if the facts presented are credible, verifiable, and consistent with other facts and information. The following are questions that you can use to determine whether the messages and facts you are receiving are believable:

- **Plausible:** At face value, does the message appear to be true and reasonable? On the contrary do the facts presented seem unrealistic or distorted? Sometime this is easier said than done, so exercising some skepticism can help you from acting unwisely on the basis of information received. If you think the message has a low probability of being true, then it probably is not.
- **Consistent:** Is the message free of contradictions? If several claims or facts are contained in a message, you have to ascertain whether or not they are compatible with each other. If you are not attentive to what the speaker of the message is saying, it's possible you'll miss key facts that could point to inconsistencies. Also consider if the information being provided is consistent with other known information not contained in the message. For example, you're told that the boss is upset with a report, but you've just come from her office and she has approved it.
- **Reliable:** Is the source of the message (the speaker) reliable? What do you know about this person's track record

for providing credible information? For example, are they known to exaggerate? If you're not familiar with the individual speaker—and as a new manager you may not be—suspend or withhold judgment until you can gather more information about him or her.

- **Verifiable:** Can the factual claims be authenticated? If the claims appear to be out of the ordinary, then verifiability becomes critical. It's okay to be a fact-checker, especially in today's environment of social media and information overload. There are so much misinformation and false claims in cyberspace, it's important to take the time to assure that information you are receiving is factual.

Sharpening you critical-thinking skills may take time, but if you learn not to come to quick conclusions about information presented, especially complex information, you'll be on the right path.

Question: Now that I'm a manager, I suspect I'll encounter more situations where I will need to negotiate. Do you have any advice about how I should approach these situations?

Answer: You are absolutely right. You'll encounter many situations such as salary issues for your staff or looking at different solutions to a problem, so having strong negotiation skills is definitely a plus.

There are a number of premises to keep in mind as you approach any negotiation:

- **Separate the people from the problem.** Simply stated, don't let personalities get in the way. Don't let your opinion of other people involved, whether positive or negative, influence your thinking. You need to identify what the problem is that you are trying to solve and stay focused on it. Admittedly, this can be a challenge if you're dealing with a difficult personality or there are too many emotions getting in the way.
- **Focus on interests not positions.** A position is a stand we take in an argument, negotiation, or conflict. It is what we demand from the other person(s)—the line we

draw in the sand. Interests are what we really want: our needs, desires, and concerns. Simply stated, interests are what will be lost or what will be gained if the problem is not solved. What's at stake? When positions become the focal point, the problem can get covered up along with any useful solution.

- **Create options or potential solutions.** When you move away from your positions, you realize that there are more than two solutions to the problems: theirs and yours. Also, the solution is not meeting the other person half-way. Problem-solving involves finding creative solutions that satisfy all identified interests—mutual or otherwise. Brainstorm to come up with as many options as possible, no matter how crazy they may seem. Don't use the brainstorming session to criticize or critique someone else's suggestion. That will stifle creativity. There will be time to evaluate. Once you've run out of ideas, only then should you start evaluating the options.

- **Insist on using objective criteria.** Before you go about evaluating the options, you will want to identify objective criteria against which each can be assessed. Objective criteria are practical, relevant, and legitimate, often based on standards, such as market value, precedent, or professional or industry standards (for example, safety or quality standards). They can be based on values shared by the individuals involved or the organization, values such as equality, fairness, and integrity.

If you're getting frustrated by a problem, sometimes it's helpful to take a break using a technique called "going to the balcony." If you detach yourself from the problem for a while, you can see it from a different perspective—from the other person's point of view. This will help you to gain clarity and use your imagination. Sometimes the best solution will come from the wildest idea.

Finally, don't get caught up in emotions. You can't escape them, but don't let them dominate. Acknowledge them, your emotions and the emotions of others, and move on.

Question: I know that I will find myself in the position of having to mediate disagreements between staff members. Are there any practical tips you can provide?

Answer: Mediation skills are essential for managers. Too many times managers try to rush in and fix every problem. In the long run, that strategy may create more problems than it solves. Taking on the role of mediator will help your team members find their own solutions to their own problems. Mediators bring an objective vantage point and serve as a neutral observer.

Mediation is an approach to resolving conflict that allows the people involved to decide on a solution rather than having a solution imposed by someone else like their manager. This gives the individuals involved in the disagreement or conflict the opportunity to express their point of view, and, more importantly, to understand the point of view of the other person. Exchanging information in a cooperative manner will only strengthen the working relationship.

You should arrange to meet with both (or all) the parties involved in the disagreement. In arranging the meeting, put the employees on notice that there is a problem, and let them know what the problem is and the impact that it is having on the workplace. Advise them that the purpose of the meeting is for them to find a solution to the problem. Be sure to get their agreement to attend and participate. You can say, "I'm happy to facilitate a discussion and arrange for a private place to talk, but I need both of you to commit to having a professional, business-like discussion."

At the beginning of the meeting, define the roles. Make it clear that you will be facilitating a discussion between them and not leading it. You won't be asking questions or giving advice or suggestions. For example, you can say:

- "I am here to help you find a solution that works for both of you, but I won't be deciding what that solution should be. I'll just help you calmly talk to each other. I won't be saying much."

- "My opinion doesn't matter. You need to find a solution that you can both agree to."
- "My role is to keep the discussion focused on the issue and encourage you to solve it."

You will also want to set guidelines at the beginning of the meeting. Let them know that each have to identify the problem and their own interests in the problem. They will have to ask questions of each other and propose solutions. It is their responsibility, not yours, to find a resolution that works.

Smart managers know that disagreements are bound to arise between staff members and they should do everything they can to prevent these disagreements from growing into larger, more disruptive conflicts. Keep the following in mind:

- Be sensitive to the working relationships among your team members.
- Encourage open communication with you and with each other. Make sure that issues are not masked or hidden.
- Gain an understanding of the interests of the parties when there are disagreements. It can help you address them sooner, and it will make you more effective if you do have to mediate any disagreements.

Question: I want to make sure that when I have discussions with other people they are meaningful and not just filled with small talk. Do you have any suggestions?

Answer: Good for you. Meaningful discussions lead to effective conversations, many of which are critical. Critical conversations occur when we talk about things that really matter and can make a difference. You will encounter them all the time in your role as a manager, such as when you're conducting interviews, discussing performance, or providing feedback—and these are just examples of conversations you'll have with your team. You will also talk about things that matter with your leadership, your peers, and business partners outside the organization.

The things that matter most in a critical conversation are time, truth, trust, and willingness to touch where it hurts the most. Let's think through this carefully.

- **Time:** Take sufficient time to deal with the matter(s) at hand. Resist the urge to convey your message, breathe a sigh of relief, and say, "Okay, we're good. Thank you." Be sure your message was received and the other person has the time to respond, ask questions, and get clarification.
- **Truth:** Be truthful no matter how difficult the message. Glossing over issues or withholding information that may be painful for the other person to hear is not helping them, it's hurting them. Respect that they can handle it.
- **Trust:** Trust yourself and trust the other person. You are both invested in this important matter and want a positive outcome. Honor any pauses in the conversation. It's an opportunity to allow both individuals to process the information that is being exchanged.
- **Touch:** Touch the issue that needs to be addressed and be specific. Be open and don't mask the issue. At the same time, recognize that you can be touching a painful point with the individual. Allow this to shape your tone and delivery.

Prepare in advance for critical conversations. Understand the information that you want to convey and receive. In giving information, be specific and provide details. Consider the information that you have that the other person might need. Be accurate and check your facts.

Any conversation involves dialogue—a give and take of information and ideas, even when those ideas are controversial or unpopular. The following can help with encouraging dialogue and receive information from the other person:

- **Being attentive,** which will help to establish ease and put everyone on an even level. Attending skills show that you acknowledge what the other person is saying and that is essential to building respect and trust.

- **Being encouraging,** which will help you draw more detailed information from the other person. You may need them to elaborate on what they've said so you can have a better understanding. It also shows that you are interested in what they have to say.
- **Being reflective,** which allows you to rephrase in your own words what you've heard the other person say and conveys understanding. If you misunderstood, it gives the other person a chance to clarify.

Finally, approach every critical conversation positively. We hear and remember positive words better than negative words and the listener is more likely to remember what you said. A positive approach will lead to a positive outcome.

Question: Emotions often run high in meetings and I get concerned that discussions can get out of control. I realize that sometimes emotions are normal, but are there things that I can do to manage these situations so that emotions don't interfere and dominate the situation?

Answer: I'm going to assume that when you refer to emotions, you mean negative ones like anger or impatience, rather than positive ones like enthusiasm and passion. It's not necessarily a bad thing if enthusiasm dominates a meeting. However, anger, impatience, or indifference can have serious repercussions.

If you're leading the meeting, you're responsible for maintaining control. Even if you're not, you can diplomatically help the leader to do so. Here are some things that should be avoided:

- Don't become distracted or allow others to do so. You want to keep the discussions on point and if other people start to veer off in different directions, bring them back. You can say:

— "You seem really interested in that, but it's not on today's meeting agenda. Would you like me to add it next week?"
— "That's an interesting point, but I'm not sure how it relates to this discussion."

- Don't allow interruptions unless it's a way to bring the discussion back to the topic, or if someone is dominating the discussion and it's necessary to give others a chance to talk. If you notice a great deal of interruptions or people talking over each other, use a tactic called a "talking stick," usually a physical object passed from person to person to signal who can speak. If you don't have the stick, you are in listen mode.
- Don't allow any one person or persons to always dominate the conversation. This will cause other people to shut down and not participate. If this is a frequent occurrence, have a signal to indicate that they have had the stick long enough and it's time to relinquish it to someone else.

Even in the best controlled settings, emotional responses are often legitimate in some situations. Controlling emotional behavior, your own or that of others, can be a particular challenge. Angry outbursts put everyone on the defensive. When you're dealing with the emotional behavior of others:

- Remain objective and focused on the issue. This is often when discussions get off track.
- Take some deep breaths. It will help you stay calm and focused.
- Model constructive behavior. Be polite and diplomatic. Use tact and exercise sensitivity toward the emotional behavior. Let them know you understand their frustration.
- Acknowledge the emotions and describe the impact that the emotional behavior is having on the discussion, the meeting, and the other participants.

- Even if you're frustrated, avoid sounding patronizing.
- Use a soft approach in responding. Soften your voice, smile, and body language. It will send a message of openness.
- Determine if the discussion or meeting can continue in a constructive way at this time. If not, propose an approach to refocus and reconvene.

The most important thing is to remember to take care of yourself. Emotions can be infectious, and it's easy to get trapped in someone else's emotions. Don't be tempted to give into their desires and demands just to get past an emotional episode. By maintaining a level head, you'll also help to maintain constructive relationships among all the members of your team.

Question: I once had a manager who was a naysayer, always squashing good ideas. I don't want to make the same mistake with my team, and I don't want them doing it to each other. How do I encourage everyone to contribute and be heard?

Answer: Nothing can demotivate an individual or group more than negative attitudes. You're right to want to avoid a discouraging working environment for your team. Recognizing this is a good first step to turning these attitudes around.

Begin by understanding that contrarianism can be positive and useful if you learn to manage it properly. Many, but not all, people who are considered to be contrarians are, in fact, visionaries. They see something that others do not see and will not go along with conventional thinking or ideas.

Put yourself on full alert when someone brings up an idea that is contrary to established norms for the group or the organization. Rather than respond "That won't work," reverse that thought into something positive. For example, you can say:

- "How would that work?"
- "What would that look like?"
- "How could we execute that idea?"
- "Very interesting. Tell me more."

By doing so, you're challenging the individual to think through and articulate their proposal or idea. You're giving them the opportunity to grow and stretch. Challenge them to come up with a plan to implement a new idea. The worst that can happen is that it fails and they learn lessons from the effort.

If another team member attempts to put the idea down, you could intervene by saying, "We've got a different point of view. I'd like to hear more." That sends the message to everyone that contributions are encouraged and valued.

There are other approaches you can take to challenge the contrarians in the group. "We've always done it that way"—a phrase that should be banned in business conversations, by the way—could be met with a very simple inquiry: "Why?" This will require the speaker to think about the current process or approach and articulate an explanation. Don't be surprised if they can't come up with one. Oftentimes, teams get rooted in doing things a certain way and don't explore if there's a better solution.

Another favorite is responding to a comment such as "Nobody does that anymore!" If you encounter this or similar comment, consider asking:

- "What causes you to say that?"
- "What information do you have that supports that conclusion?"

In both of these example responses, you're challenging the speaker, so be sure your tone and body language correspond with what you want them to hear. You're letting them know that their thoughts have been heard and that you're taking them into consideration, and that you want them to make a worthwhile contribution. If they can't be positive, then you have a golden opportunity to help them develop. The last thing you want is the person who's contrary just for the sake of being a contrarian!

A good idea needs a plan to support it. Challenging your team members when they raise ideas will help them to think critically and develop a vision of not only what can be accomplished, but how it can and should be accomplished. If you encourage them to be visionaries rather than naysayers you will build their confidence and they will be eager to contribute!

Question: How can I get my team to be accountable for their actions and their work?

Answer: Accountability is taking responsibility for your actions—owning them. It is one of those things that is easier to talk about than to do, but you're absolutely right. As a manager, you need to reinforce the importance of your staff taking responsibility—but it starts with you.

Managers should hold their people accountable for their work, but before you can do that, clear expectations must be set. One of your most important roles as a manager is letting your team know what is expected of each of them. If they are new to your organization or your team, if you're starting a new project, or if you are asking for something you've never asked of them before, they need to be crystal clear on issues such as:

- When is the task/project due?
- What are the key deliverables?
- Are there milestones for check in?
- What will success look like at the conclusion of the project?
- How will my performance be measured?

They also need to know that you are available to help or answer questions as they do their assigned work. This is one of your core responsibilities as a manager so be visible and accessible.

Once each person is clear on what is expected of them, then and only then can you hold them accountable for their work. Holding your employees accountable is not the same as micromanaging them. Set clear expectations, be available for assistance as needed, and then get out of the way and let employees do their work. If you've hired competent people and given clear direction, you have to trust them to do the work to the best of their ability. This is how employees learn and grow on the job.

As questions and concerns arise, listen to what is asked so that then next time you assign a project, you include more information. You want to be the kind of manager known for developing your employee's skills—someone who nurtures their teams so that people can be the best they can be. People want to work for that kind of manager!

If you are absolutely sure you've set clear expectations and provided the assistance needed but the employee falls short, you must follow through with the consequences. If you don't, your team will very quickly learn that you really don't mean what you say and that they really aren't accountable for their actions.

And here's the bottom line: You have to also hold yourself accountable. If you miss a deadline or make a critical error, you need to accept responsibility for your own actions. You need to model accountability for your staff.

Question: In addition to leading meetings with my staff, I may be called on to facilitate meetings with other groups or even facilitate workshops. What can I do to strengthen my facilitation skills?

Answer: Good for you for recognizing that facilitation involves more than leading effective meetings with your staff. Facilitation is a process of getting groups of people together to solve problems or explore new ideas.

Good facilitators know how to jump right in and establish ground rules or put some structure to problem-solving. They know how to lead discussions and get everyone to participate. They are good at getting to a constructive solution.

Sometimes it is best to bring in a trained facilitator, especially when the issues are highly charged and political and when people have deeply held positions. However, for good meeting management, you can learn to be a good facilitator.

At the beginning of the meeting, set some ground rules, which might include:

- One person talks at a time.
- Listen to and respect each other.
- Start and end on time.
- Maintain confidentiality.
- Guidance for taking and distributing minutes.

Once you've agreed on your ground rules, review the agenda and make any adjustments. For example, you may need to add or delete a topic based on time available. Ask a trusted colleague to keep track of time so you stay on track.

The most important role a facilitator plays is getting everyone to participate. We've all been in meetings in which one or two people dominate the conversation and the rest of the team sits quietly by. You need to ensure that everyone is heard.

The easiest way to do this is just to start on your left or right and go around the table for comments. This usually keeps the extraverts from dominating the meeting and gets the introverts involved. This takes some practice, so don't worry if it doesn't go smoothly the first time you try it.

If the discussion starts to go off track, have a flip chart or whiteboard available and jot down the topic so that you don't lose it, but let everyone know it will be on the agenda for the next meeting. If people aren't participating or are disruptive, call for a break and speak with them individually.

If the topic is something that needs to be approved before further action is taken, you can ask people to vote by a show of hands.

Closing Thoughts

Managing people is challenging work, and no one can do everything well. Find some trusted colleagues or a mentor to help you navigate the rough waters that may come up as your career progresses. Remember: Asking for help is not a weakness. Rather, it's the sign of a smart person who is looking to do their best.

Building and Managing Your Team

So MUCH HAPPENS between hiring and firing. In fact, before hiring, managers have to select the right employees, then bring them on board and set expectations and goals. Managing a team of people is a complicated process and the most important part of a manager's job. To maintain a good staff, you need to motivate them through recognition and rewards, provide feedback, and ensure that their skills are up to date. The topics in this section address these issues and more.

Question: How can I be sure I am hiring people with strong leadership skills? We seem to be struggling. Are there any suggestions or success factors you can share?

Answer: Leadership skills are such a key to having a successful team and organization, but it does take some skill to find leaders and also to convince them to want to join your organization. You may not be asking the right questions, so let's look at how you can spot leadership potential in an interview.

Successful leaders are people others want to follow because of their vision or because they inspire people to be better than they think they are. Leaders make their followers feel valued and appreciated. Leaders live their values. Leaders behave in an ethical fashion, and are caring and compassionate while demanding the best from their people. So, how do you find people with leadership skills?

Please don't start with a question such as "Are you a leader?" Any intelligent applicant is going to reply *yes,* and if you take that at face value and hire them, that's potentially a huge mistake. You have to ask a series of well-crafted questions to get to the information you need.

Here are a few you may want to consider asking:

- What values do you think you exhibit that show your leadership ability?
- Tell me about a time when you had to build support for a new initiative or project when there was resistance to your idea.
- Share a time when something you initiated didn't go right. What happened? What did you learn from it?
- What's your take on the differences between the role of a leader and the role of a manager? How have you demonstrated these abilities in your most recent job?
- What's the most important trait of a leader? Tell me about a time when you demonstrated that trait.
- Tell me about a time when you had to make a difficult and unpopular decision that impacted others. How did you communicate the decision? What was the outcome?

After you ask each of these behavioral questions, follow up with additional probes to get even more information. Ask:

- How did you do that?
- What was the result of your action?
- What did you learn?
- Tell me more about _____.

If you ask the right questions and listen carefully to the responses, you should be able to spot someone with leadership skills. When true leaders talk about their accomplishments, they use *we* a lot more than they use *I.* They know their success is not only due to their own abilities but to their skill at bringing out the best in others. That's the kind of leader that will move your organization in the right direction.

Question: Diversity and inclusion efforts are being encouraged in my organization, and I really want to get better at attracting and hiring a more diverse workforce. Do you have any suggestions of things I can do as a manager to help us with our diversity and inclusion strategy?

Answer: In our ever-changing world, organizations know that to be successful they must attract and retain the best talent, which means taking full advantage of the wide pool of applicants available in today's global marketplace. Diversity means seeking out individuals who have differing viewpoints, who come from different places, and who represent a mix of backgrounds and generations. It goes beyond traditional differences such as gender, race, or ethnicity.

A commitment to diversity and inclusion has to come from the top and be embraced and supported by your leadership, which sounds like the case for your organization.

A good place to start, as you suggest, is with recruiting efforts. You can do this by looking for candidates in places you may not have looked before. There are a number of diversity job boards and networks, such as diversityjobs.com, hirediversity.com, or minorityjobsite.com, where you can begin listing your positions. Your HR support can probably provide more examples. Don't overlook your own workforce. Ask your current employees for ideas on where to go to find diverse candidates. You'll probably get some good ideas from them.

It's not enough to hire a diverse workforce. Your organization has to be a place where uniqueness of beliefs, backgrounds, talents, capabilities, and ways of living are welcomed and leveraged for learning and informing better decision-making. This is the inclusion part of the equation.

Your organization needs to welcome people who think, look, or behave differently from others and create an environment in which they are valued and empowered to contribute. You can nurture such a culture by creating cross-functional teams, doing team-building activities, and encouraging conversations to facilitate learning about each other.

Inclusion practices need to be integrated into your communication strategies, career and professional development initiatives, recruitment efforts, and overall leadership and management practices. In other words, diversity and inclusion can't be seen as a "program" but must become part of your organization's DNA. This is key to any successful organization change effort.

Diversity and inclusion initiatives help an organization increase productivity, attract and retain talent, and provide a competitive edge in the marketplace.

Question: When I was hired, my onboarding session was mostly focused on administrative issues and it took me a long time to learn about the culture. I want to do better for my team as I bring them into the organization. I want them to start learning on their first day what we're all about. Do you have any suggestions?

Answer: You're absolutely right. A well-crafted and well-executed onboarding process is the first step toward engaging and retaining your new hires. You want them to know they made the right decision to join you, and you want them to be productive as quickly as possible. Tactical issues related to benefits, payroll, or security need to be addressed, but smart organizations leverage technology and make information available on intranets or through portals providing a one-stop information point for all these administrative issues. This not only saves time, but it avoids information overload in the beginning.

A good onboarding process starts when the candidate accepts the job offer. Use the time between acceptance and start date to communicate with new hires. Email them with things they need to know: arrival time, where to park or available commuting options, and whom to ask for when they arrive. The manager should follow up with a welcoming notice—an email, a handwritten note, or a phone call letting the employee know how happy everyone is that they are joining the team.

Consider having one of your current employees reach out to the new hire before the first day as well. Not only does this provide a sense of welcome, but it allows for a collegial relationship to form even before the start date. On the first day the new hire will know one of their peers—someone else besides the manager they can go to with questions. The last thing you want the new hire to be worrying about are things like "Should I bring my lunch, and if so where can I put it?" or "Will my cubicle have a place where I can lock up my keys or purse?"

Be ready for a new employee's first day. Have their workspace ready with all of the tools and equipment needed to do their job. Managers should plan to spend as much time as possible with a new hire on their first day. Don't book too many meetings, but if something unexpected comes up, have other members of the team available to fill the gaps. Take the new hire to lunch. (If for some reason you can't, arrange for someone else to do it.) Share the organization's history, vision, values, and mission. Please don't hand the new hire a stack of binders and put them in the conference room by themselves to read material they probably won't understand—deadly!

The onboarding process doesn't end on the first day or the first week. Build in checkpoints at thirty, sixty, and ninety days. This gives the organization the opportunity to follow up and get feedback on how the things are going. Onboarding is about making new employees feel welcome and becoming productive. It shapes employee engagement. It takes some work, but the payoff can be huge.

Question: Each of our departments has been tasked with setting goals for the department and our teams. I want to make sure that the goals are meaningful and add value but also expand their skills. I've never done this before. Where should I begin?

Answer: Ideally, organizational goals should be set by your senior leadership so that each department, manager, and employee understands what the organization plans to accomplish in the upcoming year. From there, department and individual goals should follow. Goals help organizations stay focused on what's important and keep everyone moving in the same direction. They help with employee engagement because employees want to know what's expected of them.

So, where to begin? Invite your employees into the goal-setting process. In other words, set goals with them, not for them. They will be more likely to achieve them if they are part of the process, eliminating the need to sell them on the goals. Start with sharing the organization's goals and the department's goals with you employees. Give them time to think about and draft two or three goals for themselves. At the same time, you should be drafting one or two for each of them.

You probably have heard of the SMART goal-setting process. It has been around for a long time and it still works. SMART goals are:

- **Specific:** What will be accomplished? The statement should be specific and concise.
- **Measurable:** How will success be measured? Are there metrics you can apply?
- **Achievable:** Is the goal realistic? There is nothing more demotivating than a goal that can't be reached.
- **Relevant:** Does the goal move the organization forward?
- **Time-bound:** When does the goal need to be accomplished? Are there milestones to be reached?

How many goals should you set? There should be enough to be meaningful and attainable, but not too many that will overwhelm and discourage an employee. Keep the number of goals between three and five. Try to make one of the goals personal and specific to the employee, such as completing a course of study or degree, taking a class, something that will encourage lifelong learning, provide the person with additional skills, and increase the employee's value to the organization.

Question: This organization moves quickly and priorities shift frequently. This puts a lot of stress on our teams. As a manager, what can I do to mitigate stress for my team?

Answer: I am so glad you recognize that the work environment can be highly stressful to your team—and to you as well. In addition, there's the reality that your employees are trying to balance work needs with family and life needs. You're probably not going to change the fast pace of change in your organization, so what can you do?

You've taken the first step—acknowledging that employees have conflicting priorities. Start by getting everyone together and letting them know that, though you understand they have many things going on, they also have a commitment to your organization. Let them know that you'll do all you can to help them prioritize their work and that you'll support them in completing it. Of course, this means you need to find ways to deal with your own stress so that you can be present for your staff.

Here are some simple ideas that have been successful in mitigating stress while at the same time keeping productivity high:

- Encourage your employees to take breaks during the day. Even a minute of deep breathing can reduce stress and anxiety.
- Exercise is an important factor in reducing stress. Stretch breaks can work wonders, as can short walks outside. Fresh air can be invigorating.
- Remind people about the importance of getting a good night's sleep and taking time to exercise. If you have an unused office, consider setting it up as a place for people to go for meditation or just a quiet moment to recharge.
- Have healthy snacks in the office to encourage people to eat better. Consider bringing in lunch one day, but rather than ordering pizza, order a variety of salads and fruits.
- Be as flexible as possible about time off so that employees can take care of issues in their personal lives. It will give them peace of mind.
- Recognize and reward your employees' accomplishments. It's important to keep them motivated during stressful periods.

Hopefully, these ideas will help your team get some relief from stress and also get their work done. Don't forget to take care of yourself!

Question: It used to be common practice when negotiating salary to ask applicants for their last salary or their salary history. I've seen in the news that some states have outlawed this practice. How do I decide what to offer without this information?

Answer: Smart employers are realizing that the practice of asking what a candidate was paid in their last job has resulted in some people never being paid a fair salary.

By asking what they made in their last job, you're making the assumption that their previous employer paid a fair wage, and that may or may not be true. What if that employer had a practice of paying women or minorities less and you perpetuate that practice by basing their new salary on that number?

There is a better way: Determine what the job is worth to your organization and the marketplace—because that's really what matters. You want to pay a fair wage in order to compete for the best talent. That means you have to do some research. There are easy ways to do this:

- Participate in salary surveys in your area. Many salary surveys are free if you share your salary data (and your data won't be identified by your organization's name), and they contain information that will help ensure you are competitive for similar positions. Check with the industry associations you belong to or a local HR/compensation organization for a survey that will work for you. Your HR support may be able to provide guidance in this area.
- Check public information available from Glassdoor and Salary.com for details on what jobs are worth. Be aware that your job applicants are checking those sites as well.

Once you determine what a particular job is worth in the marketplace from the research you've done, you also need to ensure internal equity—how that salary fits the other employees who do similar work. Internal equity is important, because you don't want to create problems if new hires come in a higher salary than your long-time employees.

Your decisions will certainly need to be made in light of your salary budget, but it doesn't ever make sense to underpay employees, whether they are new or existing staff. If an employee feels undervalued, you're not going to get their best work and run the risk of losing them.

Don't overlook the total rewards you offer. Do you offer a rich benefits package or a highly flexible schedule? These factors may offset lower salaries, but be sure your entire rewards program is competitive.

Bottom line: Don't ask for salary history. Pay what the job is worth to your organization and you should make job offers that get accepted and have employees who feel valued.

Question: I understand that ambiguity can compete with accountability and lead to confusion and conflict. What are some good ways to clarify expectations up front?

Answer: It's great that you recognize that at the core of many workplace conflicts is the lack of clear expectations. If people don't understand what the organization, their manager, or their teammates expect, the results can be confusion and conflict. There is a golden opportunity to set the tone early, beginning with the job interview and again at the beginning of the working relationship—the role, the job duties, and what success in the role looks like. Tell employees early about the organization's culture, letting them know that "These are our values, these are the behaviors that reflect our values, and we have zero tolerance for behavior that is contrary to our values." As a manager, you continue to have opportunities to reinforce expectations, in staff meeting and in individual meetings with your employees. In addition to establishing an understanding about what an employee's job entails, clear expectations also explain:

- How the job supports the goals and values of the organization.
- Why the job is important—how it supports other jobs in the organization.
- What good job performance means—successful outputs and results.
- The impact of good performance on others, the organization, and its stakeholders.

The following are some phrases that can help set and clarify expectations:

- "This is how your job fits into the role of the department and the mission of the organization."
- "Let's review some tasks that are part of your job."

- "If there is something you don't understand about your job, please let me know as soon as possible so I can explain it."
- "If you don't understand why I'm asking for something, please speak up and ask me."
- "It's okay to admit what you don't know."

Question: I consider myself a highly motivated person, and as a new manager I understand motivating my team is one of my most important roles. However, I am not sure how to motivate others. Where do I begin?

Answer: Motivating others is one of the most challenging responsibilities you now have. If you're self-motivated, you are ahead of the game. Good managers are role models by demonstrating their personal passion for the work, which has to be appreciated by your team members as sincere and authentic.

Motivation starts with clearly defining and sharing the organization's vision and mission. Consider:

- Have you set goals with each employee?
- Do you know what motivates each of your employees?
- Does each employee understand their role and how what they do fits into the organization's mission?
- Have you set clear expectation for the work that needs to be done?
- Are your employees held accountable for meeting objectives?
- Do you reward excellent performance?

Motivation is different for each person you manage. Some people are motivated by money while others are motivated by respect. Some want recognition while their coworker may be motivated by making a difference in the world or in their field. If you don't know what motivates each person, here are some questions you can ask:

- "What kind of work do you enjoy most?"
- "Do you prefer to work alone or on a team?"

- "What do you want to learn while on this project or in this department?"
- "How can I help you be as successful as possible?"

Today's workforce needs to know their work matters, so spend time with each staffer to educate them on the value their work brings to the organization. Sometimes, it is obvious where their work fits. For example, if they are responsible for bringing in revenue, they are well aware how what they do matters. Other times, however, it's not as obvious and you have to be creative. For example, an administrative assistant may need your help to see where their work fits but when you connect the dots for them, you may see a more highly motivated employee.

Keep in mind that highly motivated employees want to work with other good performers. This means you have to be careful not to overlook a poor performer who is dragging down the rest of the team. If one of your top performers has to constantly pick up the slack for a demotivated coworker, and you don't deal with the poor performer, you stand to lose your good performer!

Monitor your employees as they progress in their careers. Sometimes, as people stay in their jobs for a while, their motivators also change. This is where employee development becomes increasingly important. Maybe a long-time employee would benefit from being assigned to a task force or encouraged to take on a new assignment.

Motivation is a critical role of a manager and it's a difficult one so, as you build your management skills, keep your eye on your employees so that if there's a dip in their motivation, you can step in and hopefully help them regain their passion for their work.

Question: I keep hearing that my employees want to be recognized for their work. Isn't it enough that I pay them and give them good benefits? What else should I be doing?

Answer: Sorry, but it isn't enough. Your employees want to know what they do matters, and one of your most important responsibilities as their manager is to recognize them for their accomplishments.

Employee recognition is all about acknowledging that an employee did something that went above and beyond their job description or contributed an idea or thought that has wide-ranging impact on your business. Sometimes we talk about rewards and recognition as if they are the same thing. They aren't. Rewards are tangible, such as a bonus or gift card, whereas recognition is intangible.

Recognizing good performance should be one of the easiest and most enjoyable things you do as a manager. What could be more fun than acknowledging employees for doing a great job? You should do as much of it as possible because, whereas all employees want to be appreciated, Millennials don't just want it—they crave it. Because Millennials now make up the largest generation at work, recognizing their performance is a key to success in any organization.

Recognition is a great way to boost morale and motivate employees. Before you start, find out what will work for your employees. So often, leaders think they know what their employees want, and very often they are wrong. Ask your employees what would work for them.

The most cost-effective recognition and the most valued for nearly everyone is a simple "thank you" for a specific job or for completing a project or for going "above and beyond." It sounds like such a no-brainer, but you would be amazed at how few managers effectively use those two simple but powerful words. Also, consider how and when you provide recognition to employees. Hard as it is to believe, there are people who don't like to be praised in public; they would rather you quietly recognize them for their accomplishments. Don't embarrass them in public, and be sure to say thanks in a timely manner.

Besides saying "thanks," what else can you do to recognize good performance? Here are some ideas:

- Handwritten thank-you note.
- Letter from CEO or other senior leader expressing appreciation for a job well done.
- Recognition at an all-hands meeting.
- Assignment to a highly visible team or task force.

- Recognition in an employee newsletter.
- Handwritten postcards from peers who see a coworker doing something extraordinary.

Saying a sincere "thank you" may be all the recognition your employees need! Recognizing great performance is a sure way to let your employees know they are valued.

Question: In addition to recognizing our employees for doing great work, should we also reward them with something tangible like cash?

Answer: Yes, recognition is wonderful, and you should be thanking your employees all the time when they do something that deserves it, but you're right: A reward can also be a great motivator, and every time you reward an employee, you're also recognizing them. Rewards are tangible whereas recognition is intangible.

If you would like to start a rewards program in your organization, work with your leadership to put an organization-wide program in place. You need their support to fund the program and to support it! In order to encourage your leadership to support a rewards program, remind them how important rewards are to motivating, engaging, and retaining top talent. Share what turnover costs your organization. Most leaders get the message quickly when dollars are involved.

Ask your professional network or do your own research to see what works in other organizations of your size and in your geographic area. Though it's interesting to hear about what some large and hugely successful companies like Google or Facebook do for their employees, you probably aren't going to be able to replicate their programs—but they might spark an idea that you could use.

There are lots of ways to reward employees in addition to cash. Some organizations have a program in which selected employees meet with the CEO for lunch. These can be great idea-generators (or they can turn into "gripe sessions"). If you go this route, consider the personality of your CEO or leader. Are they the type of person whom employees want to get to know, or are they intimidated by the power that person holds? Consider having the HR director present to facilitate.

Many organizations still reward employees for length of service, and this can be a very effective way to acknowledge the contribution an individual makes. However, length of service awards aren't nearly as important in a world in which people change jobs more frequently than in the past. Other organizations have safety awards to reward employees for going for long periods of time without an accident or safety violation. Although these awards are great, consider more personal types of rewards programs—ones that have significant impact on the recipient and on the organization.

If you are creating a program in which prizes are given, remember that people want choice and they want items they can use in their personal life. You don't necessarily have to provide luxury items, but consider some of the programs that allow your employees to choose the gift, either online or in a catalog. That way, they get to pick something that will be rewarding to them or to their family, and if the award means something to them, every time they use the item they've chosen, they will hopefully remember it came from your organization to acknowledge something they did above and beyond their normal job.

Rewarding employees is a great way to boost morale and motivate employees, but whatever way you choose to do it, be sure your rewards programs will work for your organization.

Question: I've always believed that people need to stay at least five years at each organization and not jump from place to place. I'm finding that today's workers move around a lot more than what I'm used to. What's happened to showing loyalty toward your employer? What's the new reality for judging length of service?

Answer: Applicants used to be penalized for having a lot of jobs in a short time period, but that stigma seems to have lessened. The days when people spent a career in one organization appear to be long gone. Today's employees want to build their skills and if that means changing jobs often, so be it.

Maybe you're one of the hiring managers who used to reject resumes when you saw what was considered to be job-hopping. We thought those people were "damaged goods," had trouble working with others, or weren't committed to the work they were hired to do.

Now, it appears that changing jobs every few years is the norm—especially with Millennials. This generation believes changing jobs often is good for their career and many from older generations are agreeing with the Millennials. A recent survey reported by PayScale found that only 13 percent of Millennials think workers should stay in a job for at least five years, as opposed to 41 percent of Baby Boomers who think people should stay at least that long.[1]

People leave jobs for all kinds of reasons, but many cite a move for a higher salary as their motivator. Others leave in order to be more fulfilled in their work or to gain better work/life balance.

Another major reason today's employees move on is for the opportunity to develop their current skills. People honestly want to improve and will make a move to get developmental opportunities if their current organization doesn't provide what they're looking for.

So, if people are not staying as long as they used to, you may need to adjust your criteria when reviewing applications. When you review a resume and see that the applicant has moved from job to job, evaluate whether there was career progression. If the applicant meets most of your job criteria, why not do a phone interview and probe for more information on why they've changed jobs often. You may be pleasantly surprised at their reasons.

They may have gained valuable skills in each position that wouldn't have ever been possible if they'd stayed at the first job they had. Those skills and abilities may be exactly what you need to increase your department productivity or to take on a new challenge.

So, as you consider you own desire to see applicants with longer tenure, please think about the fact that staying longer in a job may not be a good indicator of an applicant's potential. Your best applicant may be someone who has profited from changing jobs where they've acquired new skills. Don't reject them just because they've had a lot of jobs. You may find they are more valuable to your team because they have done a lot of different jobs!

Question: We have a job opening but we're a small organization, and I'm on my own to fill the job. I posted the job on our website and have lots of resumes, but what's the next step in the hiring process?

Answer: I hope before you posted the opening you came up with a list of requirements for the position that you can now use to screen the resumes you received. Start by reviewing each resume to see if the applicant meets as many of your requirements as possible. Rarely will you find applicants who are perfect matches but prioritize them based on how closely they come to what you're looking for.

Narrow your list down to ten or so candidates that meet your requirements so that you have a manageable list to get you started. Now you need to find if what is on their resume is an accurate representation of their skills and abilities. It is disappointing that, according to CareerBuilder, 75 percent of HR managers have caught a lie on a resume, so you need to take the next step: talk to candidates.[2]

Contact each candidate by email to set a time for a screening interview. Most organizations still do screening interviews by phone but there's a growing trend of doing them via Skype, Google Hangouts, Zoom, Facetime, or other platforms in which you would ask the same questions you'd ask on the phone. There's also a trend to ask the applicant to video themselves answering the same questions you'd ask in a screening interview.

There are advantages to using video because more than one person can hear the responses—either they'll be with you when you do the Skype interview or when you share the video responses with others in your organization. The downside of using technology is that some of your applicants may find it uncomfortable or don't have easy access to it. In that case, the phone screen works just fine.

In the screening interview, you'll want to confirm information on the resume and ask some open-ended questions such as:

- "Why are you in job market now?"
- "What was it about our job announcement that caused you to apply?"
- "When are you available to start a new position?"
- "Briefly describe your last or current job responsibilities."
- "What salary range are you looking in?"

At the end of the screening interviews, thank the applicants and let them know your timing for completing a hiring decision. For example, "We are doing a series of interviews in the next week and will be making a decision by the 15th as to who will be invited in for an in-person interview. Of course, this is all based on business pressures. I commit to you that we will keep you informed throughout the process." Do your best to keep candidates informed so that they have a good impression of your organization—even if they don't move on to the in-person interview.

Be sure to read the next two questions, which have additional information about interviewing candidates.

Question: I am filling a key position in my small organization. After conducting screening interviews, I've narrowed the candidate pool down to the top three people and now I need to bring each one in for an interview. Should I interview them myself or ask some of the other department heads to join me when we meet the candidates?

Answer: Our advice is to conduct individual interviews with each candidate. It is much less intimidating for the candidate to meet one on one. The interview can be more conversational in tone, rather than when the candidate meets with a group of people at once, all of whom ask them questions.

Although it takes additional time and coordination to do separate interviews, the quality of information collected can be worth it.

Some organizations, such as the federal government, use what's commonly called a "panel interview" almost exclusively. This is the kind of interview in which the applicant meets at one time with several people who each take turns asking questions. There are several advantages to doing panel interviews: They save time, they're easier to schedule, and all the decision-makers hear the same information at the same time.

So, it's really up to you as to which format works best for your organization, but no matter what please coordinate what each interviewer is going to ask. Nothing turns an applicant off quicker than when everyone asks the same questions. Have each person who will be participating in the interview process focus on a different part of the job or a different skill required.

If you chose to do a panel interview, let the job applicant know before they arrive for the interview, and give them the names and titles of who will be on the panel. If you're asking colleagues to do individual interviews, try to schedule them on the same day. Then, send the applicant an itinerary with names and titles. Don't forget to build in time for breaks, especially if there is a full day of interviews scheduled. One great idea is to have the department the candidate would be working in if selected, have lunch with the candidate. This is a good way to get additional feedback on the candidate from people who will not be on the interview schedule.

No matter which format you use, prepare questions ahead of time, and make them open-ended and applicable to the job candidates are interviewing for. There is a simple formula for developing good interview questions:

- Tell me about a time when you _____.
- Give me an example of when _____.
- Walk me through _____.
- Describe for me _____.

Once you've asked the open-ended question, you can continue to get more information by using probes such as:

- How did you do that?
- What did you do with that information?
- What did you learn from that experience?
- Tell me more about _____.
- How so?

Meet with the other interviewers and get their input on who best can do the job. Check references on your top candidate and, if all's well, make a job offer. Don't forget to send a well-written message to those you interviewed but didn't hire, but hold off doing so until your offer is accepted.

Question: I've worked hard to build a good team and we're working well together, but I know our top performers are vulnerable to offers from our competitors. I don't want to lose them. What should I be doing?

Answer: As you consider how to retain your great team, ask yourself these questions:

- **Do they know how much I value them?** This is sometimes referred to as "re-recruiting your superstars." Think of what you did initially to interest them in working for your organization and for you personally, and do some of those things again. Sell them on the value they add to your team and let them know you are committed to adding to their skill set.

- **Do I know each person's career goals?** When you are clear about their goals, you can provide them with opportunities to build skills in those areas. Great employees crave learning experiences such as mentoring, so it's your role as a manager to help them achieve their career goals.

- **Am I providing the high performers with career development opportunities such as mentoring, conference attendance, seminars, or degree opportunities?** Investing in your superstars can encourage them to stay with you. Employees, especially Millennials, want to learn and grow, so be sure you offer development opportunities.

- **Do I acknowledge good performance with recognition in a way that is meaningful to each person?** Some people respond to public recognition of good performance; others would rather you just tell them in private.

- **Am I rewarding my great performers in ways that will motivate them to stay with me?** In order to do this, you need to really know them individually so the reward will fit them personally. To some people, a day off is a great reward. Others would rather have a bonus. Still others may prefer the chance to take on a new and challenging project to build their skill set. There are countless ways to reward performance, but it isn't a "one size fits all" proposition.

You probably do exit interviews when someone resigns, and you can learn valuable information from those interviews, but if the person has already resigned, you can't use that information to make any changes. So, try talking to your employees when they're still with you. Sometimes this is called a "stay interview." Ask about the plusses and minuses of working for your organization. Ask them to tell you if they plan to leave you in the near future and if there are things you can do to keep them a little bit longer. Ask them to describe a great day at work or what they would change about their job or you as their manager, if they could. Be prepared to take action on the ideas you hear from them. If you can't implement a suggestion, let the employee know why you can't or else they'll never give you another suggestion—*ever!*

Be sure your great employees know how much you value them. Give them the feedback they crave and, whenever possible, reward them with not only recognition but with work that will develop their skills. If people feel as if they're learning and growing, odds are they'll stay right where they are.

Question: I really want my team to innovate more. They do good work, but rarely have new ideas or process improvement suggestions— and I crave new thinking and new approaches to how we accomplish our goals. How can I encourage them to be more innovative without sending the message I'm not satisfied with their work?

Answer: I love that you want to encourage innovation, but do your employees know this is what you want? Do they know you are totally open to new ideas and suggestions on how to improve processes? Unless you tell them, they're probably not going to actively share their ideas so get the word out that you welcome their input.

Then enjoy it when the ideas start flowing in and be sure you carefully consider every one. If it isn't possible to implement a suggestion, close the loop by letting people know why their idea or suggestion can't be used. If you don't, you may not ever get another suggestion!

Generating a new idea takes time and effort. Your employees need to know that you value their creativity, so acknowledge their idea and give it careful consideration. Please don't ever say, "We tried that ten years ago and it didn't work." Even if that's true, a lot has changed in ten years and maybe it will work this time. Don't just dismiss an idea quickly. That will totally shut down the idea flow you so want to encourage.

Keep in mind that many people get stuck doing the same thing they've always done and may need a reminder that being creative is valued. You can encourage your staff to experiment with tasks or come up with ideas for changing a work process by asking questions that challenge the assumptions your team may hold. If you want them to explore new ideas, you may need to use more than words to get them started.

You may want to consider a contest to collect great ideas—a good way to get many at one time. All you need is to announce it, set a time frame for suggestions to be submitted, and attach some sort of reward for the best idea. Put a committee together to evaluate the suggestions, and award the best one something simple like a gift card to a local restaurant. Another way to generate ideas is to create an "innovation team" and let the ideas fly!

Some organizations solicit ideas using the "suggestion box" method that allows people to make suggestions anonymously. However, this method doesn't allow you to reward or recognize a good idea, nor explore it further, unless the person self-identifies.

If you're serious about wanting your people to be more innovative, be sure your culture encourages taking risks. If your teams aren't comfortable stepping out and suggesting a new way to do things, no matter what you offer, you won't get what you're looking for.

To encourage innovation and creativity, make it easy and comfortable for people to come forward with new ideas. Reward and recognize them for their ideas appropriately—remember that not everyone wants public recognition—and let them know how receptive you are to hearing what they think.

Question: I want to encourage my employees to continue to learn and grow. What can I do to help them see the importance of continuous learning?

Answer: Lifelong learning is a phrase you hear a lot in today's business world, and for good reason. Just as you've discovered, no matter how high any of us rises in our careers, we always need to be adding to our knowledge base and our skill set. In today's highly competitive world, it is critical for everyone, managers and employees alike, to be expanding and growing their abilities.

Some leaders think they have to know everything in order to be respected, but that's hardly the case in our ever-changing world. Start by modeling the behavior you want to see in your employees. When your team sees you adding to your skill set, at least some of them will want to follow your lead.

Share what you're learning with your staff. You can do this by taking a few minutes in a staff meeting to share a book, article, or other resource you've found to be helpful. If your employees seem receptive, it is a great idea to ask everyone to read a particular article or watch a specific video and then discuss it when you next meet. This is an easy way to get your employees interested in expanding their knowledge or skill base.

There are so many ways to learn using available technology, including:

- Webcasts.
- Podcasts.
- YouTube.
- Online articles.
- Audio books.
- TED Talks.

Some managers maintain a resource center, with books and articles available to employees to borrow. You could also work with other managers in your organization to set up an organization-wide library.

An easy idea to encourage learning is to select an article or book that everyone reads. Then discuss the major themes during your weekly staff meetings—a great way to build your team's knowledge base but also your team's cohesiveness as they learn together.

Don't overlook the massive open online courses (MOOCs)—online courses presented by some of the most respected, major universities and by companies including Coursera and Udemy. MOOCs are an easy and reasonable way for your employees to obtain knowledge from respected sources at a time that works for them.

Mentoring is another way to encourage lifelong learning. It used to be that mentors had to be older, more experienced employees but now a mentor can be anyone who has knowledge or a skill someone else doesn't possess. You can use your current employees or subject matter experts from other parts of your organization to share their knowledge or skill and this costs your organization nothing. Mentoring also can be a great way for your team to work with others in your organization and learn what they do.

There are many ways to encourage lifelong learning. When you do, you are not only building their skills, you are also helping your organization gain a competitive edge in your market so this is one of the greatest win-wins you'll ever have.

Question: I want to get to know my employees better and encourage my team to get to know new members better. However, I don't want to cross any lines. Any suggestions on how I can start a conversation that's appropriate for the workplace?

Answer: It's great that you recognize that there are boundaries and don't want to cross them. Boundaries and individual privacy are eroding, and it's unfortunate because those invisible lines that help define roles and manage interpersonal relationships at work.

It's also important that you get to know the people with whom you work. It's natural to be curious about each other and explore our differences and similarities. Having a curious conversation with someone has to be organic and genuine. You don't want to appear to be purely nosey.

One way to begin these conversations is to share something about yourself. Doing so exposes some of your own vulnerability, but it also lays the foundation for asking questions. There are a number of ways that you can start these conversations. For example:

- "I grew up at a different time than you did. I'd love to hear more about your experiences, but let me share some of mine first. These are some of the events that influenced my life."

- "I spent most of my childhood in a large city and had some really interesting experiences. Can I tell you about some of them?"
- "We're going to be spending quite a bit of time working on this project and it's inevitable that we'll learn things about each other's life. For example, in my time off, I like to spend time outdoors. What do you like to do?"

Keep in mind, however, that some employees may be reluctant to share much, especially with their manager. That's okay. Don't push them to disclose. Also, people have different ways of communicating and sharing. For example, an extrovert may be direct, forthcoming, and open with information about her background and personal life, whereas an introvert may be more reluctant to share information with anyone.

There are some things that are not appropriate for sharing in the workplace, such as gossip or employees' personal issues (e.g., problems with spouses/partners or personal finances). If an employee seeks to confide in you about these, you should refer them to your organization's Employee Assistance Program provider or to your human resources support. If you become aware of your employees crossing boundaries with each other, take the opportunity to caution them against doing so. It's not the basis for respectful relationships and it's clear those are the type of relationships that you want to foster among you team members!

Question: I know that giving employee feedback is important, and I've been reading that feedback should be given often. I want to make sure the feedback I give is useful. Are there any secrets to giving effective feedback?

Answer: You are very astute to realize that your employees want feedback that is useful. How and when to provide employees with feedback are at the core of performance management. It is a powerful motivator, but to be effective, feedback must be ongoing and frequent. Employees want to know that they are making valuable contributions. That's what motivates and retains them. They also want to know if they can do things better. Think of feedback as giving both praise and advice.

To be effective, feedback should be timely—given at the point in time when something happens. If an employee does something outstanding, let them know as soon as you observe it. It will motivate them to do more outstanding things and reinforce their positive behavior or performance. Conversely, if there was something an employee did that could have been done better, let them know right away in a constructive and candid manner. For both praise and advice, be sure that you are conveying:

- **What you are recognizing:** the performance or behavior that is or is not working well. This should include any expectations that are or are not being met. Be specific and give examples.
- **What impact the performance or behavior had on the organization or others, and whether that impact was positive or problematic.** Don't be vague.
- **What the future holds:** changes to be made or continued improvement and the consequences of both.

Feedback should always be given in a positive, communicative atmosphere that encourages dialogue between you and the employee. Remember that they may have some thoughts about how they are performing, and this is a good opportunity to get their perspective and bridge any gaps that may exist.

Having regular discussions with your team members gives you a tremendous opportunity to give and get input. Consider developing some questions to facilitate these discussions. For example, ask each team member:

- What they see working and what they see should be continued.
- What they see as not working well and needs to change.
- What they can do more of in order to be effective, and what can you do for them to increase their effectiveness.
- What are some of the specific actions they will be taking in the short term to address the above.
- What assistance you can provide them.

Feedback is often not much different than solving problems, so the more the employee is engaged and a part of the process, the more effective the solution is likely to be. If you approach a negative situation as criticism rather than an opportunity to advise, the outcome is likely to be undesirable for everyone. Always consider what the employee will get out of the information you provide and focus on things that he can do something about ("I'd appreciate you keeping the team informed about the status of the project," for example). Finally, in these situations, give feedback in calm, unemotional words, tone, and body language; and be sure that your message was clearly heard.

Question: My team seems to be faltering about its purpose and it is affecting the members' ability to work together. What are some things I can do to help strengthen them and make them more cohesive?

Answer: Teams are critical for most organizations, especially when their goals and objectives are too complex to be accomplished by individuals working independently. The key, then, is to have high-performing teams that have clarity on issues such as mission or purpose, roles and responsibilities, and values that drive behavior.

Teams usually go through differing stages of maturity as they form and grow. Of course, as things change, such as new members joining, old members leaving, or new leadership, those stages can change and even regress. Try doing the following to bring you team back to focus.

- **Mission:** The team's mission or purpose must support the organization's purpose. Individually, then collectively, ask the members to come up with a motto for the team that reflects the organization's mission. From the suggestions, have the team clarify their mission.
- **Roles:** Understanding who must do what is important to the team's success and can reduce the potential for infighting. However, this is often rife with confusion. Ask each team member to individually write down their responsibilities, then share with the group. Don't be taken aback if individuals are surprised what they learn

from their colleagues. It's an opportunity to reinforce where lines of responsibility lie.

- **Behavior:** Behavior within organizations is embodied in its values, and those values provide the guide for behavior throughout the organization. Bring your team together and have them develop norms for how they will work together (for example: active participation by all team members, demonstrate respect for all viewpoints by not discounting others, cultivate a variety of options and a commitment to deadlines). Let them identify behaviors that contribute to as well as deter from high performance.

An important aspect of highly functioning teams is that the members collectively and individually are accountable for results and outcomes. To strengthen their accountability, have the team collectively discuss common concerns and set ground rules around these concerns. Some common concerns and issues teams often have include:

- How members interact with each other both in group meetings or face to face. For example, if a rule is no interruptions when someone is speaking and interruptions occur, how will they be handled?
- What happens if obstacles prevent assignments from being completed on time? For example, how will they be addressed? To whom and when must notifications be made?
- How decisions will be made. If a consensus cannot be reached, for example, what is the fallback position?
- When conflict arises, how will the team manage it? What process will be in place to prevent the conflict from driving a wedge between members? Will the team view conflict as a potential source of creative energy?
- If confidentiality is breached, how will the breach be addressed?

From your question, it sounds as if your team is at a point where they need you to facilitate discussions around the issues presented in this question. Once they develop a better sense of their purpose and become comfortable operating as a team, you can become more of a catalyst to them. Let them push their boundaries to see beyond the status quo to what they can be and accomplish!

Question: How can I address my employees' desires for work-life balance with my business requirements?

Answer: Here's another difficult issue that involves you as a manager listening carefully to your staff while you monitor productivity for your organization or department. It is not impossible to have a highly productive organization that honors the fact that the people who work hard to make things work also have lives outside of work.

Technology has had a significant impact on this issue—both positively and negatively. Technology allows us to work anywhere and anytime, and that can be really great or really bad for employees. We hear people complain that their manager sends emails on weekends and late at night, making them feel they have to be available 24/7, and if they're not, it will have a negative impact on their careers.

But, we also know that when people are not given time off to rest and relax, that can have serious implications for their health, relationships, and their overall happiness.

Here are some things you can do as manager to help your employees have work/life balance while keeping productivity high:

- **Offer flexible work schedules.** Whenever possible, let your employees work from home a day or two a week. As long as the work gets done in a timely manner and to your requirements, cut your people some slack on when they need to be physically at your place of work.
- **Watch for burnout.** Monitor energy levels, attendance, or participation in meetings. See if you notice someone who is usually the first to volunteer for a special project suddenly holding back; it might be a sign they're overwhelmed.

- **Disconnect.** Give your staff permission to not respond to emails between certain hours or on weekends (and refrain from sending messages during those times unless it is an actual emergency!).
- **Encourage people to take time off.** We've all heard the alarming statistics about how many Americans don't use their vacation time because they're afraid they won't be seen as totally committed to their work. Everyone needs breaks to refresh and rest, so let your people know you want them to take time off and here's where you can model what you want them to do. Take your vacation time and use weekends to disconnect yourself. You will be amazed at how creative you are when you are away from work pressures.
- **Encourage a healthy lifestyle.** Have healthy snacks available in your workplace and encourage your employees to exercise regularly. Some organizations subsidize health club memberships while others have "walking clubs" that take walks during lunch breaks.
- **Take breaks during the workday.** Even a five-minute break to walk around the block can help an employee focus better when they return.
- **Use your Employee Assistance Program.** Bring them in to teach meditation or mindfulness, which can help keep stress at a manageable level.

Encouraging work/life balance is a recruiting and retention tool as well and that's good for your bottom line!

Question: I know that at some point as a manager, I am going to have to terminate an employee. What are some of the things I should be thinking about and should be doing before I actually have to end someone's employment relationship with the organization?

Answer: It's very admirable that you realize that you may have to confront such a situation during your management career and want to be prepared for it. Likely your organization has policies that address employee behavior and employee performance. Employees are generally terminated for cause when they are not meeting the expectations of how they should behave at work or performing the requirements of their job. These policies will describe the protocols to take when expectations are not being met. It's important that you understand these policies and if you have questions, discuss them with your human resources or legal support.

Keep written records regarding employee performance and behavioral issues. Not only will this help support a termination decision, this documentation can be helpful if you leave your current role and someone else replaces you. Keep records on an ongoing basis, as incidents occur. Document any informal warnings and counseling, even for minor issues.

Anytime you have a discussion with an employee about breaching a rule of conduct or not meeting a performance standard, write it down. Capture a summary of what happened during the meeting, including what the employee was told and any objections that may have been raised. Good documentation—and good preparation for the meeting with the employee—should include:

- **Facts.** Use only factual, job-related information and avoid speculation. The conduct or behavior should be accurately described, including the sources of information (such as your observations).
- **Objectives.** Detail those performance and behavior expectations that the employee failed to meet. Explain it in a constructive way.
- **Solutions.** Describe any assistance, coaching, or guidance provided to the employee, including any specific suggestions provided to help the employee reach established objectives and improve.
- **Actions.** Clearly articulate the steps you are taking now and those that you will take if objectives are not met or behavior does not improve.

Your organization likely has a process for termination decisions to be reviewed and authorized by more than one level of management along with human resources and/or legal staff. Before you present your recommendation to terminate an employee, examine the situation and consider the following:

- Has the employee violated a policy or practice? If so, was the violation serious?
- How has the organization dealt with similar violations in the past? Has your department dealt with past violations in a manner consistent with the organization's practices?
- How long has the employee worked there?
- Has the employee been involved with policy violations in the past?
- What is the employee's performance history?
- Are there mitigating circumstances?
- Have any federal, state, or local laws been violated that require specific action?
- If claims of harassment or discrimination have been made, have they been thoroughly investigated by the appropriate parties? Has all the evidence been examined?
- Have you reviewed all of your documentation and given the employee the opportunity to change their behavior or performance?

Hopefully, your earlier discussions and counseling with the employee will avert the need for any adverse action. If not, and the employee's poor behavior and performance persist, your documentation and examination of the situation will support your decision and allow you to implement this action with confidence and dignity.

Closing Thoughts

Managing a team can be challenging for any manager, but if you have the right people in the right jobs and set clear expectations and provide ongoing feedback, your team should accomplish what your organization requires of them. Watch for dips in productivity and step in to motivate your team to want to do the best job possible, but don't overlook where their stress points are. Today's employees deal with many challenges, so keep your eye on each team member and make changes if needed.

Creating Your
Personal Brand

ONCE YOU ASSUME the role of manager, all eyes are on you. Beyond knowledge and skill, you have to show that you are credible, competent, and trustworthy to be a successful manager. How you present yourself, how you communicate, and how you act all reflect on the type of leader and person you are. The questions and answers in this section reflect on those traits that project confidence, credibility, and integrity.

Question: I understand that creating a personal brand is important. I expect the discussions in this section are inspiring. How do I encapsulate, protect, and maintain my brand?

Answer: Your brand is important. It helps to define who you are as a person and a manager. Acting consistently and with integrity is one of the most important things that you can do to preserve it. When people know they can count on you to act in a certain manner in every situation, you gain credibility and their trust. You are known as someone who can be relied on to get things accomplished and produce results. As you conduct yourself in your personal and professional life, remember:

- Always be true to your values and principles—your belief system. Although you may share certain values with other people, yours are unique to you. Honor them and use them as your guide. Make decisions that demonstrate your values and never contradict them in your actions or words.
- Seek out people with common values. They will bring out the best in you and be a source of sound and ethical advice. To the extent you can, avoid people who don't share the same high standards as you and don't tolerate behavior based on lower standards. Never allow other people to contradict your values.
- Always act with self-confidence—don't second guess yourself—and leave yourself open to new ideas and opinions. Maintaining an open mind does not erode your self-confidence. It helps you grow.
- Maintain a high regard of respect for yourself. You cannot respect other people if you don't respect yourself first. Never tolerate actions by others that disrespect you or anyone else. Speak up.
- Respect the people around you, your team members, peers, and leadership members. Demonstrate respect by being on time for meetings, not interrupting, and acknowledging others when you see them, for starters. Never disparage the leadership in front of others. If you disagree with something, speak up. If you have to vent (and we all do on occasion), do so privately and to someone who will listen and keep your confidence.
- Always lead by example. This is not a cliché. It's a practice that should guide your behavior. Other people will notice, especially your team and they are the ones who are likely to follow and behave similarly.
- Avoid being judgmental. You'll make mistakes and so will everyone else. It's fine to counsel others, but refrain from criticism.

- Exercise discretion at all times. Don't engage in speculation or gossip. Never discuss sensitive business information in public places or spaces (at restaurants, at bars, or
  on public transportation, for example). You never know
  who is listening. Wait to make or return phone calls until
  you can do so in a private place.
- Respect and keep confidences unless, of course, there is
  a need to disclose such as information about wrongdoing like harassment or something similar that could pose
  significant risk for the organization. If that's not the case,
  honor your commitment not to share it with anyone.

Integrity and respect should be the cornerstones of your brand.
Always put ethics at the forefront. Hard work goes into building your
brand, so you're wise to protect it. It will serve you well throughout
your career.

**Question: I've heard other people say that it takes courage to be
a manager, but I'm not sure what that means. How do I as a manager exhibit courage in the workplace?**

Answer: Being courageous is a critical component of being a manager. Courageous managers are the people who earn the trust of others and who succeed where others fail. A manager who is courageous
doesn't keep his or her head down and go along with everything and
everyone. One way to show courage is to be comfortable speaking up
when you think a peer or member of the senior management team,
including the CEO, is about to make a strategic or even legal mistake.
Courage in the workplace means having the integrity to speak or act
in situations in which you know the organization is heading in the
wrong direction and may be unwilling to change.

Don't be afraid to respectfully confront situations you think are
wrong or need improvement. Present alternative options when you
believe options are being overlooked. Strong leaders surround themselves with people whom they consider advisors—people who are
competent and don't shrink from telling the truth, especially when
they think a leader is wrong. Be secure in your own abilities and

knowledge to speak up. People who provide a different point of view, or explain why they think something needs to change, exhibit courage and integrity.

Confront wrongdoing that you observe, even if it is occurring outside of your chain of command. If you hear about wrongdoing second-hand, report it to the appropriate resource in the organization. Don't be afraid about stepping on toes. It could help avoid legal or public relations risk.

Courageous leaders will not only speak out, take an opposing point of view, or confront situations and bad decisions, they will also suggest and advocate for ideas and positions that may be unpopular. They are not afraid to put the interests of an employee, their team, or even the larger organization above their own self interests. They move beyond the "what's in it for me" mentality, sometimes to their own detriment, because they have the vision to see greater, long-term outcomes.

Courageous managers also solicit feedback from their teams. This starts with getting to know your people. Listen to them, take advice, and act on sound recommendations. Be willing to admit what you don't know. Encourage staff to offer ideas, comments, and criticism, and don't allow other team members to filter information, even if it's bad news. You should not filter information from your team, unless that information is confidential or proprietary.

If you maintain a climate of openness in which everyone is comfortable speaking up and bringing information and ideas to you, or soliciting your ideas, you'll gain respect and show that you have the courage to lead your team.

Question: I intend to be the best manager I can be. Can you share some best practices or resources for me to up my game?

Answer: You probably know that there are a lot of books, webinars, podcasts, YouTube videos, and so much more available to you with tips on how to be the best manager ever. Here are a few of what we think are the best strategic actions you can take:

- Don't make the mistake of pretending you know all the answers. Too many managers think if they admit they don't have all the answers, they won't be respected when, in reality, the opposite is true. Letting people see that you're human actually gains you respect and loyalty from your team. Be ready to apologize when you've made a mistake and take responsibility for the actions of your direct reports.

- Get to know the people you manage. Know them well enough to understand what motivates them, what encourages them, and what's important to them at work. This may be difficult for some people who aren't comfortable with the interpersonal side of work, but this is a critical step to being a highly respected manager.

- Be a good listener. Focus full attention on the people who speak to you and listen with the intent to learn—not to respond. You'll be amazed at the knowledge you'll gain by listening to your people and you will build their self-esteem, which will make them more successful.

- Reward successes and learn from failures. Too many managers don't stop to reward success or recognize outstanding work from their employees but are quick to point out what people did wrong. It's good management to learn from what went right or wrong on a project, and it is also good to celebrate when good things happen.

- Be a positive role model. Live your organization's values in a way that lets your staff see you really believe in your mission and you uphold good business practices. People want to work for managers they respect, and nothing will lose you respect faster than violating one of your organization's values.

- Provide developmental opportunities for all your employees. No matter how high someone rises in the organization, they can always use skill-building, and this includes you. Model your commitment to employee development by improving your own skills. Be a lifelong learner!

- Find a mentor inside or outside your organization who can give you good advice and feedback and, while you're at it, encourage your employees to also look for mentors.

Following these steps will help you become a better manager, but don't ever stop adding to your skill set as a manager. Check out the Resources section of this book for good sources of additional information on becoming the best manager you can be.

Question: I've heard that successful managers think like entrepreneurs. If that's true, how do I do that?

Answer: Your question indicates that you've already begun to do so by thinking outside of the box. One way to approach this challenge is to consider the characteristics that make a good entrepreneur. These include the following (and there are certainly others):

- **Visionary:** They spot opportunities and act on them. They may have a keen eye for detail and, if they are running a business, they have to pay attention to them. However, they look beyond the micro level and see the big picture. In your day-to-day duties as a manager, this may mean seeing opportunities for your team members (for example, developmental opportunities, such as stretch assignments). It can also mean looking at new processes and procedures—new ways of doing things.
- **Risk-Taker:** Successful entrepreneurs are deliberate and calculated in making decisions about those risks. They will look at the costs and benefits of taking the risk. If you are considering a new process, for example, will you gain greater efficiency, if it is implemented? Conversely, will greater efficiency result in a reduction of staff?
- **Decisive:** Once they have weighed the advantages and disadvantages, entrepreneurs make a decision and move forward. You are going to implement the new process, reallocate duties, and give all staff members the opportunity to assume new responsibilities. The department can now take on new projects.
- **Non-Complacent:** Entrepreneurs are never satisfied with the status quo. They are always learning from the past—mistakes and successes—and making improvements.

What was successful about the implementation of the new process? Can you replicate it for another process? What would you do differently? When will you analyze the new processes effectiveness and make any necessary adjustments? These are the questions an entrepreneur will be asking.

- **Tenacious:** If difficulties arise, entrepreneurs don't get discouraged or walk away. They are persistent, looking for ways to make it better, and are not willing to give up easily. If the new process isn't working quite the way you envisioned, you don't abandon it. Rather, you'll explore why and solicit ideas about how it can improve.

- **Curious:** One of the reasons entrepreneurs are not complacent and are tenacious is their curious nature. They want to understand more about what is going on around them and they have a great capacity to explore new things. They love to ask questions as a way to learn more. As a manager, the more curious you are about your staff, and about the how and why they do things, the more you'll learn.

Entrepreneurs bring a great deal of clarity to their vision. When they embark on something, there is no ambiguity. They are purposeful in their endeavors. Everything is intentional, even if the intent is to learn and explore. Finally, they are great at networking. They seek out people and groups with whom they can connect and because of their curious nature, they can elicit interesting and useful information and build meaningful relationships.

Question: I've been really surprised about the countless rumors that appear to be circulating among my team members, most of which are untrue. I'm overhearing most of this gossip and I'm not sure how to address it. I'd like to just ignore them and hope they'll stop. Should I take any action?

Answer: Not only are rumors unproductive and disruptive in the workplace, you're risking your personal credibility by simply ignoring them. You are right to consider taking action. As a manager, you want to send a strong message about integrity, and you can do so by confronting the rumors and setting the record straight with facts. Be proactive rather than hope the rumor mill will stop operating. One thing you can do is to address the rumors in a staff meeting, which not only provides the opportunity for everyone to ask questions, but it also lets your team know that you value open and factual communication.

Establishing and maintaining your personal integrity as a manager are so important to your success. Some things that you can do personally to promote an ethical work environment are:

- **Treat everyone with fairness and respect.** Show respect by always paying attention and listening, such as when others ask to speak with you or when others are speaking in meetings. Give your undivided attention, refrain from reading emails, and don't take or make calls unless it's an emergency situation.
- **Walk the talk and set a good example.** The proverb that actions speak louder than words is real. You team is watching, so act in a professional and respectful manner at work. Be purposeful in your actions and choose your words wisely.
- **Exercise discretion.** In addition to avoiding gossip, keep confidences to the extent you can. If someone wants to tell you something in confidence, let them know up-front that if what they tell you will put the organization or another person at risk, you will have to disclose it to others who have a need to know. However, if that's not the case, honor your word. Don't discuss issues about your employees (for example, issues related to wrongdoings or discipline) with other managers or team members.
- **Don't speak disparagingly about others.** No matter how frustrated you may be about something or someone in the organization, express your views with care. Don't lash out at a colleague, a team member, or someone in leadership. Find a trusted source, preferably outside the

organization, if you need to vent. If you disagree with a policy, tell the leadership in a positive, in-person conversation. If you're disappointed in someone, talk to them face-to-face and let them know why.

Question: This is the year I want to move forward in my organization. What should I do so I can position myself for career growth?

Answer: Before you start thinking about getting promoted, be sure you are doing the best job possible right now. It's easy get complacent while you focus on your next career move, but you'll never move up in your organization if you aren't at least a solid performer in your current job! Better yet, you need to be consistently exceeding expectations so that when you ask to take on new responsibilities or to move to the next level, your organization will consider you for the job.

Once you're sure you are exceeding expectations, volunteer for additional assignments where you will gain visibility in your organization. Is there a task force you might serve on? Is there an interdepartmental project you could volunteer for? If you do get to be on a task force or do a special project, do great work there while keeping up your current responsibilities at a high level.

Research the kinds of experience, knowledge, skills, and education the job you want requires and put together a plan to match up the requirements with your background. Your HR department should be able to help you evaluate your skill set as compared to the job requirements.

If your organization offers career development webinars, podcasts, training programs, or any other way to gain new knowledge, be sure you take full advantage of what's offered. This is also a great time to seek out a mentor in the area you'd like to work in, and gain knowledge and experience from interacting with your mentor. You can also offer to be a mentor to someone else in the organization. Take advantage of your education reimbursement program, if offered, to complete your degree or add a certification that may be important for the position you want.

If your firm doesn't offer employee development opportunities, you can still build your skill set. There are lots of free webinars available, and don't overlook YouTube and TED Talks as free but excellent sources of skill-building opportunities. Look for articles and books that will add to your knowledge and put you in a better position to be promoted.

Once you're sure you are as prepared as you can be, talk with your manager and get feedback on whether you might be a candidate for the next opening. If you hear that you need to gain experience or develop a skill in a particular area, take that feedback to heart and continue to prepare yourself for the next level.

Question: Our organization has had some ups and downs recently, and I sense some of our staff aren't firmly in our camp. I really want my employees to trust me and our organization. What can I do to build trust?

Answer: I hope what's been happening in your organization hasn't been too difficult or hasn't made its way into the press, because if and when organizations or managers don't live their values or do what they promise to do, trust goes right out the window.

Trust can't be demanded. It must be earned over time and through consistent behavior and actions. Rebuilding trust is even more difficult but critical to your organization's success, because when trust is broken productivity usually suffers.

We know that employees want transparency. They want to know what's happening in your organization and/or department and they want to know the good, bad, and ugly. So, start by being honest with your team. Of course, there will be things you as a manager know about that will not be appropriate to share, and you will get more comfortable with these issues as you grow as a manager. For example, if layoffs are being discussed, you would not want to discuss this with your employees until final decisions are made and you've been trained in what to say and how to say it.

One of the best ways to build trust is to listen to your people. Spend time getting to know each of your direct reports, and listen carefully to their questions and comments. If your organization does employee surveys or focus groups to measure engagement, pay close attention to the results and take action when appropriate.

Being consistent is a great trust-building strategy. Your employees want to trust you so keep your word. If there is ever a time when you can't do what you promised, let your team know why and do it quickly. Sometimes there will be issues out of your control so share why you couldn't keep a commitment and move on.

Admit when you're wrong. It is hard to trust someone who isn't secure enough to admit a mistake. This is a difficult lesson for many managers who don't want to appear not to know everything. But, no one knows everything and there will be times when you make a mistake so learn how to "own it." A heartfelt "I'm sorry" goes a long way to building trust.

Never bad-mouth one of your employees to another team member! This is a surefire way to destroy all you've done to build trust.

Never ask an employee to tackle a job you're not willing to do yourself. In fact, a great way to build trust is to work alongside your employees on a project so that they see your commitment to them and to your work.

Always give credit where credit is due. Recognizing good work done by your team is a great way to not only build their skills and their confidence but their trust in you. And, it probably goes without saying, but don't ever take credit for something you didn't do!

Building trust is not a one-time event. You will be working on this your entire management career and it is well worth the effort.

Question: I work in an organization that works hard to support a positive culture. Even with quality programs and policy, disruptive behaviors occur. What can I do, personally, to keep such behavior to a minimum?

Answer: It's clear that you already realize that as a manager you play a big role in influencing the quality of the climate in your organization. There are a number of personal initiatives in which you can engage, starting with how you act, react, speak, and conduct yourself at work. Remember that your team and others are watching, so always act professionally, and be respectful and purposeful in your actions. Choose your words wisely.

- Refrain from engaging in joking and teasing, especially if the comments could have the effect of disparaging others. There is a thin line between joking and harassment.

Though it might be tempting to laugh at every joke or comment you hear, think before you respond.

- Don't ignore such comments. You have the responsibility to assure that the behavior doesn't get worse, so respectfully confront the individual(s), explaining why such a joke or comment is wrong (for example, "You may intend that joke to be funny, but it's belittling and demeaning").

- Always confront and act on any behavior that you observe that is discrimination, harassment, or bullying. If you receive reports of such behavior, act on those as well. Depending upon the nature of the reports, act in accordance with your organization's policies. You may have to take corrective action against one of your employees, or notify either your legal or human resources support about reports you've heard.

- Be proactive. Talk about disruptive behavior of all types in meetings with your staff. Let them know that such behavior won't be tolerated (for example, "Emails and comments that take aim at coworkers are not professional and need to stop" or "Comments and jokes of a sexual nature don't belong in the workplace").

- Have open conversations about the organization's policies with individual employees and in staff meetings. Listen to their concerns. Let them know that they are empowered to report harassment and discrimination to you, legal, or human resources without fear of retaliation.

- Encourage your employees to discuss any behavior they feel is inappropriate at work with you—even if it's not behavior that could be discrimination or harassment. Less severe behavior can quickly erode if not addressed. Let them know that they are empowered to report harassment and discrimination to you, legal, or human resources without fear of retaliation.

- Take responsibility to assure that the policies and protocols your organization has in place are, in fact, working appropriately. If you hear they are not, let your senior leaders know so it can be determined why they aren't working.

Being proactive and taking action when disruptive behavior occurs not only maintains the organization's positive culture, it also builds your personal trust and credibility. Your employees will have confidence in you and the organization, and be proud to be a part of it.

Question: Our organization is committed to having a culture that is inclusive and respectful of everyone. I want to set a good example for my team members about the importance of diversity. Knowing that words matter, do you have any guidelines on using the correct terms and language to avoid offending anyone?

Answer: You are so right: Words do matter. It's not only the choice of words, but the tone that is used to convey the message. It is so important to choose your words carefully.

Language is symbolic, meaning there is an arbitrary connection between the symbols (words and phrases) and what they refer to. Stated another way, different words and phrases can have different meanings to other people, depending on their perspectives and experiences. In today's diverse workplaces, communication can be complex and challenging!

Formality is changing significantly in today's work environment, which is becoming more casual. Determine the level of formality within your organization. Is it acceptable to address people by their first name regardless of age and/or position? Whatever the norm, let new employees know what's expected. Rather than be stymied, the simplest solution is to ask someone what they liked to be called or how they like to be addressed.

Be wary of slang, jargon, acronyms, or insider expressions that come about through shared experiences, including shared experiences within the organization. It can make a newcomer, an external consultant, or a service provider feel like an outsider. If these terms are used, be sure to translate them so everyone has the same understanding.

Avoid words and phrases that may be offensive and keep in mind that acceptable terms and phrases can change. Use neutral words or words that are comparable (for example: black or white, gentleman or lady, man or woman). "Girls Night Out" could be acceptable if the comparable activity would be "Boys Night Out." However, I'll have "my girl" get back to "your girl" is totally unacceptable. Imagine if you said, "I'll have 'my boy' get back to 'your boy'! It should go without saying that any slang term for an ethnic group is not acceptable in the workplace, even used by someone from that group.

Don't use labels. You usually do not need them unless you are describing a person when physical appearance is essential. In that case, just state facts (about six feet tall, dark complexion, short beard, shoulder-length hair, blue jeans, red jacket, etc.). If you must use a label, refer to the person first and the descriptor second. The Americans With Disabilities Act is purposely not called the Disabled Americans Act. People are individuals first, not their disability.

Remember that communication is an important way to build positive relationships at work—with your team, your peers, and your managers. Paying attention to what you say and how you say it is an excellent way to start. However, keep in mind that you may say the wrong thing at times, or say the right thing in the wrong way. If that happens, don't berate yourself. Apologize, learn from your mistake, and move on.

Question: I understand that words matter, but actions and body language speak as well. What else can I do to model positive behavior that supports diversity and inclusion?

Answer: Fair treatment and inclusion of all employees does go well beyond words. There are so many examples of people not being included evenly. For example, in meetings all members are not polled for their opinions. Certain people are allowed to dominate. An idea comes from a woman and is ignored; it is repeated slightly differently later in the meeting by a man and is complimented/accepted. Be mindful and respectful of everyone present, even if you are not running the meeting. Acknowledge what everyone has to say. Remember that it is okay to gently interject if you notice someone is attempting to speak and someone else is dominating.

Gestures and expressions can often convey powerful messages. Negative messages can be sent through eye rolls, smirks, or other expressions of disinterest, such as listening with arms crossed, or looking at watches or electronic devices in meetings while others are talking. Don't tolerate this type of behavior from your team. It has the effect of devaluing other individuals by negatively impacting feelings of inclusion and self-esteem.

Diversity includes many types of differences from introverts and extroverts to ages and backgrounds. Keep in mind that treating people fairly is not the same as treating them equally. People are individual and unique, and each individual may need to respond or be treated differently in a given situation. It's not the easiest job for a manager, but it's an important concept to keep in mind.

Watch people's reactions. How are they receiving information from conversations? Private conversations might be necessary to understand preferences. Some people need more time to process information. Their great ideas may come hours after the meeting has concluded. Invite everyone to submit comments, thoughts, and ideas in writing as well.

If people have good ideas, achievements, and contributions, acknowledge them publicly, unless that is embarrassing to them. If so, thank them in private. Know how they react. The best managers give credit where credit is due and address shortcomings in private when necessary before they grow into big problems. Abide by the old saying "Praise publicly; reprimand in private."

Finally, the most important compliment you can pay someone is to listen to them. Yet listening is probably the most misunderstood communication process we use. Be conscious of your listening habits. Make a conscious effort to hear what other people are saying. Turn off your listening filters and sharpen your listening skills.

It is good business to treat all people with respect, and this is reflected in an organization's profitability and its ability to attract and retain the best employees. If employees feel valued, their contributions to the organization will continue to grow over time.

Question: Now that I'm a manager, I know it's important to become a better listener. I'm trying to improve my listening habits and improve my skills. Any tips on what I can do?

Answer: Listening is probably the most misunderstood communication process we use. It takes some focus and patience, but if you are committed to sharpening your listening skills, it can be done. And, your better listening skills will not only be useful at work, they will help you with any relationship!

Let's start with what listening isn't. It's not, when the other person is talking, waiting for your turn to talk. If that's your approach to listening, that means you probably aren't even hearing what the other person is saying. You've focused on preparing what you're going to say when they finish!

Listening is hard work for most of us, and we've spent little time learning how to listen. A good listener makes a deliberate effort to understand the other person's message. A good listener listens to learn, is interested in what the speaker is saying, and lets the speaker know they're listening.

If you're serious about being a better listener, consider what's called "active listening." It's the most powerful way to capture the entire message the speaker is attempting to convey. Here's how it works: While the speaker is talking, the active listener encourages the speaker to share by nodding, maintaining eye contact, a raised eyebrow, or a smile. These cues let the speaker know you hear them and want to know more. However, you have to really mean it. If you aren't sincere, the speaker will probably not want to continue to talk to you!

Another active listening technique is to paraphrase what you heard the speaker say (e.g., "I heard you say that my department needs to respond more positively to requests from your staff"). Then, if that's not what the speaker intended, the information can be clarified—but they will know you were listening!

As you work to improve your listening skills, consider what gets in your way. Maybe you're distracted by external noise or other people. If so, when you find yourself in that situation, ask the speaker if you can move to a quieter location. Maybe the timing is bad. If you're on a tight deadline and can't focus, ask if you can postpone the discussion until you can give it your full attention. Also consider any cultural barriers or differences that may get in the way of understanding. Maybe the speaker uses words or phrases you don't understand. If that's the case, ask for clarification.

Listening is such a critical skill, and we can learn to listen with the same amount of energy and enthusiasm we use when we talk. Yes, it takes additional work and concentration, but the payoff is great!

Question: I've been told that as a manager I should improve my accuracy in reading nonverbal communication. Why is reading non-verbal cues important and how can it help me better communicate?

Answer: Communication is more than just being articulate when you speak, more than just being able to write an outstanding report, and more than just listening with your ears when someone is talking. It's about relating to the other person or group of people. If you're not paying attention, the other person may state they understand, but their tone, facial expressions, or body language may be conveying a different message. You have to be able to read all the nonverbal clues you are receiving.

Nonverbal communication is important because it's an indicator of:

- The effect you are having on others.
- Whether or not you are getting your message across to others or if you are understanding their message.
- Other people's emotions and emotional state.

Being able to observe other people, especially when you are engaged in a direct conversations or encounters with someone, allows you to be comfortable. When you are comfortable with one another, you are able to relate to that person and track their ability to follow you. The result is that you are in sync with each other; you are communicating.

What exactly should you be observing?

- **Tone of voice:** Is it warm, natural, and personal, or formal and stilted?

- **Facial expressions:** Are their eyes rolling, teeth clenched, and brows furrowed, or do they have bright eyes and wide smiles?
- **Body language:** Is it stiff and stoic, or animated? Are they slouching or sitting on the edge of their chair?

In this process of observing others, you will learn to better read behavior and get a better sense of what the person is feeling. You will become more empathetic. Empathy is important because the other person may be reluctant or unable to express their feelings, especially to their manager. However, as a manager, it's important that you know and understand those feelings.

- Does their face express anxiety or enthusiasm over the news about a new project assignment?
- Do they respond warmly or angrily regarding the new team member they'll be working with?
- Does their failure to make eye contact mean they're ignoring you or processing what you are saying?

Certainly, if it's a negative message you're getting (anxiety, anger, or indifference), that's your cue to further explore the situation. If you miss these cues, you could be setting the other person or the team up for some difficult times. This is an opportunity to understand any underlying issues.

Communication is a two-way street. When you are communicating with someone, you have the responsibility for making sure your receiver gets the message you are sending. So don't just speak, communicate with your whole expressive self. Show through body language and expression how emotional you are about an idea or issue.

As a manager, the more you perfect your ability to read and send nonverbal cues, the more confident you will be in your impressions of people and your ability to assess them. As you learn to appreciate subtlety in messages, it will help you better understand each member of your team—what each person is capable of—and make good decisions about the work you all need to accomplish.

Question: I've heard that emotional intelligence is just as important to professional success as technical ability. Can you shed some light on this?

Answer: Emotions have a big impact in our interpersonal relationships with others, and they greatly affect our ability to work efficiently and harmoniously. We spend a great deal of time at work, so we want that time to be positive. Emotions, whether positive or negative, can be infectious. As an example, say an anxious or angry team member seeks your help, but their emotion has the effect of making you become more anxious or angry, impeding your ability to help them with the problem.

Too often in the workplace, there's an expectation to leave feelings at the door, but feelings and emotions are normal and natural human traits. It's important that you are aware of them and your ability to express them in a constructive way. That's where emotional intelligence comes in.

Emotional intelligence is a person's ability to recognize their own emotions, understand them, and realize that their emotions affect others around them. It also includes a person's perception of others—understanding how they feel. People with a high degree of emotional intelligence are keenly aware of their own emotions and don't let them control their actions or get out of control. They harness their emotions (a passion for excellence, for example) and put them to work for positive outcomes. Emotionally intelligent people can not only manage their own emotions but can influence the emotions of others. They are good at recognizing the feelings of others and thus can have a calming effect on them, making them less angry or anxious, for example, in a tense situation.

If you want to strengthen your emotional intelligence, here are some considerations:

- **Be mindful of how you interact with and react to other people.** Do you rush to make judgments before you have all the facts? Are you aware of your biases? Are you open and accepting of differing views and perspectives?

- **Be aware of how you react in stressful situations.** Do you become upset when things don't go as planned? Do you blame others?
- **Be aware of how your actions affect others and put yourself in their place.** How would you feel or react? Would you want that experience?

When you find yourself in a particularly tense situation with someone, a team member, a peer, or even your boss, the following should help:

- Maintain a level-headed response to other people's emotions.
- Don't let them push your buttons and get you riled up.
- Be understanding. The other person may be deflecting emotions toward you and not the situation.
- Acknowledge their emotions but let them know the effect they're having on the situation or conversation.

All of the qualities of a highly emotional intelligent individual (self-awareness, self-regulation, empathy) make the emotionally intelligent person a good listener and excellent at managing relationships, which are essential for managers and leaders.

Question: I'm finding that as a manager I need to compose more emails. What can I do to make sure they are clear and effective?

Answer: Most written communication today is taking the form of email, so your staff and leadership should be grateful that you recognize it's important. Because email is not interactive, it lacks the subtleties of face-to-face or telephone communication—nonverbal clues such as tone or body language. So getting your messages right is important. There are appropriate circumstances to use and avoid email.

Use email when:

- Your audience must get the message.
- Multiple people must receive the message.

- Your audience is at a distance. (It's simple, practical, and economic.)
- A quick but not instant response is needed.
- Time is needed to compose the message.
- A record of the message is required.

Avoid email when:

- An immediate response is needed. Not everyone checks email regularly or has constant access to email, and some individuals procrastinate.
- Text alone is not powerful enough. Sometimes dialogue is needed or you can't risk the message being misunderstood.
- The information is sensitive, such as bad news, or you need to convey confidential information.
- You are angry or agitated.

In addition, there are protocols for email usage to which you should adhere. These include:

- Understand the difference between "To" and "CC." The more people you send an email to, the less likely any single person will respond or take action. For multiple recipients, address (To) the message to the ones who need to take action. Copy (CC) those people who may have a need to know.
- Use the subject line, but don't discuss multiple subjects in a single message. The subject line conveys the substance and importance of the message. If it's blank, the message may end up in a spam folder. If you need to discuss more than one subject, send multiple emails.
- Use greetings and closings, such as "Dear (Name)" and "Best Regards." This sets the tone and level of formality and puts that final considerate touch to your message.
- Keep messages brief and to the point. Be concise without being abrupt. Make your most important point first,

then provide any necessary details. Be clear why you are writing. Keep paragraphs short and use plain, simple English. If the message is too long, it's likely to be overlooked and you won't receive a response nor the action you are seeking.

- Be mindful of your tone, because the subtleties previously mentioned are not present and the message can be misinterpreted. The more matter-of-fact you can be, the better.
- Use a signature and be sure you include your contact information (phone number and address) so that the readers can get in touch with you in a suitable way. Some may prefer to call rather than respond to your message.
- Never write in all caps, the digital equivalent of shouting. Besides, it's harder to read.
- Reread your message before sending it. Sometimes your fingers move slower than your brain, so you want to be sure your message is clear. Use your spell checker and grammar checker to catch any mistakes.
- Finally, remember that any email messages that you send are business communications so treat them as such. You may be more casual with your friends, but these are your staff, colleagues, and management reading your correspondence. You want your emails to be received in a professional manner!

Question: As a new manager, I'm concerned that I may not always have the answers to all the questions I'm asked or a solution to every situation that arises. I don't want my team and peers to lose confidence in me. Any suggestions about how to handle these situations?

Answer: Nobody likes a know-it-all, so stop fretting. You're not a manager because you have all the answers to everything. Rather, it's because you can plan and organize work, hire the right people to do it, and make sure it gets done. Don't be afraid to show your vulnerabilities.

Start by recognizing your limitations and admit them to yourself. If there is an area that's critical to your team in which you're weak, make sure that you have someone who's strong in it. Don't be afraid to admit, "That's not something I'm particularly good at. Would you mind taking responsibility for this?" In doing so, you'll demonstrate not only your honesty, but your confidence to admit you are not an expert at everything. You also send the message that you recognize your team's expertise.

Next, admit to yourself that you don't know everything and get comfortable with that. Things are constantly changing in today's business environment, and you will encounter new things and plenty of gray areas. It's okay to admit you don't have all the answers. Face it head-on and ask others what they think. Consider saying:

- "I've not experienced that, have you? How did you handle it?"
- "I don't have the answer, but let me try to find out. Perhaps we can work together to figure it out."
- "I don't know, but let me put you in touch with someone who does."

If you don't understand something you are told, don't pretend you do. Ask for clarification. If you're not clear about something, don't assume. If you act on an assumption and you're wrong, you'll not only look foolish, you'll risk damaging your credibility.

Finally, admit and learn from your mistakes, and share those lessons. If your team is faced with a challenge similar to one you've encountered, they will be delighted to hear you say, "Let me tell you about a time I faced something similar and really messed up!" They will appreciate your candor and willingness to share what you learned so they can avoid a similar mistake.

When mistakes occur, whether it's your own or a member of your team's, take responsibility and don't assign blame. Assess the damage and offer some solutions; this can be a team effort if appropriate. Apologize to those affected by the mistake and let them know you're taking steps to prevent future occurrences. Then take steps to make sure it doesn't happen again.

Don't waste time and energy trying to make others think that you are perfect. You have limitations, cannot answer every question or fix every problem, and have made mistakes. You're not perfect, you're human. Your ability to spotlight your vulnerabilities will increase your credibility and gain the respect of your team, peers, and leadership.

Closing Thoughts

Your personal brand is a key to your career success, and it's something that should always be developing and evolving. It lets people know what they can expect from you—that you're approachable, fair, ethical, or decisive, for example. Your brand sets a standard of respect for you and your organization, and an example for your team to model. Nothing and nobody can ever negatively affect your personal brand!

Managing Up, Down, and Around

KNOWING HOW TO get things accomplished in your organization is key to managing. To do this, you have to understand what other departments do, how they operate, and what standards they have in place. You have to develop collaborative relationships throughout the organization. Finally, you have to recognize the role external partners may play in helping the organization achieve success. The discussions in this section will provide you with greater understanding of these issues so you can manager effectively.

Question: I seem to be spending a great deal of time answering questions about benefits, personal leave, vacation requests, training opportunities, payroll, expense reports, travel arrangements, and purchasing new equipment. It's getting frustrating. Am I expected to know the answers to all of these issues?

Answer: It's no wonder you're getting frustrated. It sounds as if your team members are expecting you to know everything. The sign of a good manager is not necessarily knowing the answers to everything, but rather knowing where to send people to find the right information.

Certainly any manager should be able to answer inquiries about time off for vacation or other personal leave. You've got to make sure that the work is getting done, and you can't have everyone away at the same time. If employees are asking about the organization's leave policies or benefit programs, you may want to direct them to human resources or to your employee handbook.

Requests about training opportunities may be an employee's way of starting a conversation about their professional development, which is certainly a conversation you'll want to have, or at least begin. Both you and the employee may need to seek guidance from your human resources support about available sources that will meet any of the employee's development needs. This would be valuable information for you both to know. Ultimately, you've got to approve the time and budget for your team members' training. The same is true for requests about purchasing new equipment. You're responsible for the budget and you should understand any procedures for purchasing equipment. You may need to coordinate purchases with other departments, such as IT, as well.

Other requests about issues such as payroll, expense reports, or travel arrangements should be directed to the appropriate department. It's possible that the information that is being conveyed isn't clear or readily available. Many organizations establish intranets, through which various departments can provide information about their policies and processes. If this is the case in your organization, make sure your employees know how to access the information.

If a new policy, from any department, is issued, be sure that it's communicated clearly to your team members. New policies can often be confusing, so be sure you have a way to field and consolidate questions, and get back to your team in a reasonable amount of time once you have the answers.

Question: I recognize that I've got responsibility for managing my own team and encouraging all the members to work together in a collaborative fashion. In addition, I recognize that I'm part of a management team and I want to work collaboratively with my peers. Do you have any suggestions about how I can go about doing this?

Answer: It's great that you've recognized that you are part of more than one team in your current organization. Having strong collaborative relationships with your peers is so important, because no one person or department stands alone. In today's organizations, work is interdependent, and you cannot afford to stay in a silo.

Begin by seeking out your peers and invite constructive feedback. Find out what the pain points are. In other words, what do your internal customers expect from your department, and what have they been receiving and not been receiving? It's important that you understand what other departments need from you, especially if you manage a support department, as well as how your department is perceived.

Once you've received this feedback, determine if the expectations are realistic or not. If they are not, it's important to communicate back to your peers why not and determine how more reasonable expectations can be set. They need to know the realities under which your department operates. For example, if you manage a staff function, there's a tendency to always want to respond to the C-suite first. You need to determine if this is serving the organization well. Talk to peers who manage other staff functions and get their insights.

Explore common business interests with your colleagues. Determine how you can support the work of each other's operations and what the benefits are for each of you for doing so. If you agree on action items that you can each take, develop a plan to do so that includes follow-up. Then, be accountable to each other for completing those items.

If there are common issues that you are struggling with, explore how you can work together to address and/or solve it. If you are new to the organization, or even to your role, respect that your peers have institutional knowledge that they can share with you. These are the people who can tell you what the practices are around certain areas and where you can find additional information about policies and protocols. As you build mutual trust, they are likely to be more candid with your than perhaps your manager might be.

Meet regularly with your colleagues. Have breakfast or lunch—whatever fits your respective schedules. Use these opportunities to learn as much as you can about other departments, which is especially important if you're new to the organization. This will also give you both the chance to explore what factors are working to help you collaborate and how you can build on those factors. Don't just talk business. Recognize that you all have interests outside the organization—and you may share many of the same personal as well as business interests. This will help build trust and comradery!

Question: I've had wonderful people during my career who served as mentors and helped me get to the management level. I'd like to start a formal mentoring program and have the support of senior management to do so. Can you give me some ideas how to get started?

Answer: Good for you to want to "pay it forward" and encourage mentoring in your organization. Mentoring is an excellent tool to develop staff that doesn't cost much (or any) money but can pay huge dividends for the individual and your organization, including your ability to hire talented employees. Smart job applicants ask if they might have a mentor to help them be more productive if they join your organization. Other benefits of mentoring programs include the development of cross-organizational connections as people mentor employees from other departments and build channels of communication—often between people who might not have otherwise worked together.

When designing a formal mentoring program, consider these things:

- **Goals:** They must link to the organization's strategic goals or a specific developmental goal and be clearly defined.
- **Leadership support:** Like any initiative, you need to have top management support for the program to succeed. This may be as simple as having your CEO kick off the program or as complex as getting budgetary support to provide resources for mentors.
- **Customization:** The program must be specific to your organization and/or department. (Don't copy someone else's program.)

- **Support:** Mentors should be trained and have resources available as needed. Some organizations provide recognition for mentors or time off to compensate for the extra time they spend on mentoring others.
- **Selection/matching:** Decide who is eligible to participate in the mentoring program, how you will select mentors, and how you will match them to mentees. Not everyone is qualified to be a mentor. (See the bulleted list that follows for what makes a good mentor.)
- **Time period:** Determine if the program is open-ended or is for a specific time period.
- **Evaluation:** Include a way for you to measure effectiveness of the program so that you can improve/revise as needed.

Don't forget to consider the qualities that you want in a mentor:

- Someone who has knowledge or skill in an area that you don't have.
- Someone who is a good listener.
- Someone who has a genuine interest in developing the skills of others.
- Someone who is trustworthy.

Some people think that mentors have to be long-term employees who've had lots of organizational experience. In reality, a mentor is anyone who has knowledge or experience that the other person doesn't have.

Finally, do not discount the fact that mentoring can also happen organically and informally when an employee approaches someone and asks for guidance over time. Even if your formal mentoring program doesn't get implemented as you envision, you can always encourage employees to seek out mentors on their own. Because this is a passion of yours, be sure to use your expertise to mentor others!

Question: Someone in my department just saw a great deal on equipment we need at a local big-box store. We could save a significant amount of money purchasing it there, but we have to use our organization's vendors. Any advice for convincing the

procurement department to stop exclusively using their preferred providers and vendors?

Answer: Being cost-conscious with the organization's money is admirable, but understand there's generally a good reason that certain providers have been chosen. These decisions are not made lightly nor arbitrarily. Chances are a fairly rigorous process to choose each provider and vendor was used, and if you're ever in need of specific products and services, you will probably have to work closely with your procurement department. The process for choosing vendors usually includes the following steps:

1. **Research:** During this phase extensive research is conducted, wherein needs are analyzed and goals are established. Potential costs are also analyzed, and the cost of the goods and services should be included in your annual budget. It is not unusual to also conduct a cost-benefit analysis if you're looking at services to make sure they can't be provided cheaper internally and to determine the return on investment. Procurement is dependent on the department requesting the goods and services during this initial step because they will be the primary users. The research should also include a review of the marketplace in order to identify potential vendors and providers.

2. **Request for Proposal:** A request for proposal, or RFP, asks vendors and providers to propose solutions and pricing that fits your needs, but also assures consistency in responses so they can be easily compared. RFPs typically asks for the following information:
   — An executive summary or synopsis of the provider's goods and services, and their understanding of your needs.
   — Company information, namely size, financial stability, business viability, and experience.
   — Deliverables, or how they will meet your needs.
   — Project team and resources.
   — References.
   — Cost.

3. **Evaluate Proposals and Select a Provider:** During this step, providers will be evaluated based on the strength of their proposals and possibly site visits to their establishments. In some cases, potential providers may be invited to make presentations to your organization. Elements of the evaluation include, at a minimum, scope of resources and ability to meet your needs, quality of product/services, reputation (which is generally based on references), value-added capability, previous or existing relationship, flexibility, cultural match, and cost. Members of the department requesting the goods or services play a big role in evaluating providers.

4. **Contract Negotiation:** This usually is the responsibility of the procurement department, with input or oversight from the general counsel or outside lawyer since the contract forms a legal obligation. The contract will include, but not be limited to, key deliverables, time frames, payment terms, and performance standards.

Question: I have an acquaintance who works for a local media outlet. She often asks if I would talk with her about developments in the industry. Are there any reasons that I shouldn't let her interview me?

Answer: It may be perfectly acceptable for you to talk to the press, but before you do anything, you should be very clear about your organization's policies and ensure that your response is aligned with anyone else speaking on behalf of the organization. Matters in the media often involve the reputation of an organization: why you met certain performance goals or didn't, why you enacted or retracted a specific policy, what you did or didn't do to support your customers, why you are hiring or firing a top executive, and so forth. When speaking to the press, the well-being of the organization must take absolute priority over individual egos or personal agendas, which can sometimes be hard to ignore. The response must be objective, deliberate, and considerate.

Even in times of significant crisis or a minor misstep, which many organizations experience, the top concern in any response must be in preserving and protecting the reputation of the brand of the organization. This is especially true when tweeting or posting video. These can go viral and dramatically alter or derail an organization's agenda for months or sometimes even longer. The media and the public can also tell when an organization isn't being completely forthright in their response. This is especially true if multiple people are speaking on behalf of an organization and presenting alternate stories or conflicting points of views. This only fans the flames of curiosity and makes people want to dig for the "deeper truth," which can cause unnecessary headaches and distractions and deplete your brand currency in the marketplace. Each organization has a finite amount of what we call brand currency in the public eye, which can either be used to promote or defend its reputation. You want to be very judicious in where and how you spend it. Matters of the media are best left to the organization's representatives who are best versed in this arena. It's not about censorship, but about preserving the integrity and image of the brand and preventing any significant or long-term damage.

Question: I hear the term "risk management" used often, but I'm not sure what it means, especially in my organization. Is this just a new term for workplace safety and security, or is there more to it?

Answer: You are certainly right that workplace safety and workplace security are both big parts of risk management, but as you suspect, it goes far beyond—and both of those areas have expanded greatly. Concerns about employee health and safety, or environmental health and safety as it was often called, have evolved into risk management systems that also include concerns about individual and organizational security and privacy.

A big part of health and safety involves compliance with the Occupational Safety and Health Act (OSHA). There are a number of standards to which organizations must comply, as well as injury and illness reporting and recordkeeping requirements. (You can read more about OSHA at *www.dol.gov/compliance/laws/comp-osha.htm.*)

As a manager, you should understand the procedures in your organization for reporting any accident or illness. Many organizations, even those in the non-manufacturing sectors, have safety management programs, which may conduct ongoing worksite analysis to identify potential safety and health hazards so preventative measures can be implemented and/or corrective actions can be taken. Employee health and wellness programs are another integral part of risk management. Depending on the structure and size of an organization, these programs are often overseen by human resources, facilities, or another administrative function.

Workplace security covers a broad range of subjects designed to protect an organization from numerous threats. Security programs require an integrated approach, involving organizational entities such as human resources, facilities, security, finance, IT, legal, and public relations, as well as outside consultants specializing in risk management and Employee Assistance Programs.

Under the umbrella of security, physical workplace security plays a big role. Access to buildings and facilities (security guards and structural or electronic barriers, video surveillance, badging, or other identification systems) and protecting physical assets against harm or theft are widely recognized aspects. Physical security also includes response to threats such as workplace violence and natural disasters, including evacuation plans, such as fire drills.

Beyond physical security, risk management also includes protecting an organization's confidential and proprietary information. This can include policies and procedures about the appropriate use, disclosure, and discussion of information and access to computer information and employee data. Organizations take great care to prevent identity theft—theft of personal information of their employees and customers. Cybersecurity is an area in which risk management works closely with IT to prevent hackers and cyber criminals from gaining unauthorized access to computers, networks, and data.

A final area of responsibility that falls to risk management is emergency preparedness. Emergency preparedness and response programs define the steps to be taken during and immediately after an unexpected or violent incident occurs. Risk management must keep crisis management plans current. They must also develop continuity plans to ensure the organization can withstand disruption.

As a manager, you should be familiar with your organization's risk management program and any protocols that are in place to support the welfare, safety, and security of your employees and the organization.

Question: Technology is drastically changing the way work gets done. I have some ideas for process improvement in my department. How and when do I get IT involved?

Answer: Technology certainly can make work more efficient and you're wise to be thinking about process improvement. However, before you rush out and ask IT to design something, there are a number of issues that you will need to consider and some actions you will need to take.

Determine the desired outcome and the impact that outcome will have, especially on employees. For example, are you looking for efficiency so staff members have time available to perform more strategic work? If so, how will you prepare them to take on more responsibility? What type of training might they need on new, automated processes? What resistance might you encounter?

Conduct a cost-benefit analysis to ensure that an automated process would be cost-effective. If so, then with IT's help, determine if there is already an off-the-shelf software that will meet your needs. Will an off-the-shelf solution need to be customized? If nothing is available and a solution needs to be built, does your IT support have the resources to do so? What type of technology support (e.g., online reference guides) might be needed if a new process and technology solution are implemented?

If something does need to be built or developed, you will need to explain what it is and be involved in the design. You will need a work-flow analysis, in which you examine each task that is performed, focusing on activities that happen again and again. Be sure to capture every step in the process, including beginning and ending points. Provide as much detail as possible, no matter how small those details may seem. Elicit input from your team—the people who are actually performing the work. Though this may sound tedious, it will help you to understand each step and you may even be able to identify some that are unnecessary—or some that could be added. It will also provide a good road map and facilitate your discussions with IT as you share the process and your thoughts for improvement.

When you sit down with IT and explain your needs, find out early in your talks if they have the knowledge, skills, and time to design and develop the new process, and provide continuing support if necessary. If the project moves forward, commit resources from your team or department so the people involved in doing the work contribute to the design of a new process. They will provide great value when it's time to implement the change because they've been part of it from the beginning.

Question: My organization is very entrepreneurial, and everyone is encouraged to be aware of new business opportunities, even if their role is not in sales. Are there things I should know about sales and marketing so I can support the growth of the organization?

Answer: It sounds as if your organization has, or wants to have, a sales culture, and it's great that you want to embrace it. One of the first things to recognize is the distinction between marketing and sales.

Marketing is the process of planning, pricing, promoting, and distributing the organization's goods and services. The marketing function is often research-focused, determining the needs of the customer base and the organization's ability to meet those needs through the products and services it has, or can develop, and its capabilities of making them available. A good marketing function builds lasting relationships with both customers and suppliers, which is commonly referred to as customer relationship marketing.

Sales, on the other hand, is responsible for selling the products and services of the organization to the marketplace. The sales function depends on the research and data provided by the marketing function when planning its approaches and strategies.

It sounds as if your organization places a high value on building lasting relationships, which is a great business strategy. Businesses that rely on cold calls or contacts, in which success is measured by the number of answered calls or opened emails, are not aligning themselves for sustained growth. These efforts can have a negative impact on the organization and its image. Organizations that take a customer or client relationship approach recognize that all of its team members represent the interests and values of the organization. Even if you're not directly involved in selling, there are some skills that are essential to sales that will help you:

- **Strong personal skills:** qualities such as passion, energy, self-motivation, integrity, and the ability to work across the organization to understand and serve the customers, clients, or members in the case of non-profits or member-based organization.

- **Strong relationship skills:** qualities such as humility, ego control, confidence, and personal responsibility. Don't forget these related skills of building collaboration and listening. Relationship-building has to occur within the organization as well as with external stakeholders. Just as team members want to work with other great team members, potential customers want to do business with people, not with an impersonal organization that relies on cold calls or contacts.

- **Excellent business acumen:** an awareness of the total business environment. The ability to understand the needs throughout the organization coupled with the needs of the potential client or customer. Understanding the client's needs builds relationships, which builds trust, which helps sell not only an organization's goods and services, but the integrity of the organization itself.

Sales may not be your official job within your organization, but remember that in your day-to-day interactions with clients, customers, or anyone outside your organization, when you're conversing, handling objections, networking, building relationships, listening, and helping, you are using the fundamental skills of selling. And most of the time you don't realize it! When you speak, people form an impression very quickly, and that is a selling activity. It's also the basis for relationship-building. If a potential opportunity presents itself, bring in the sales professionals. You can still be part of the process, especially if capabilities need to be defined. This is a good way to build internal relationships. When you build relationships, internal or external, you build trust. It's a message no manager or leader can ignore.

Question: I know there are a great deal of demands in any workplace today, but getting assistance from our support departments, like IT or facilities, can be frustrating. Any suggestions on how I can get their attention when either I or one of my team members need their support?

Answer: You're right to be frustrated at times if you can't get an immediate response to a call for help, but keep in mind that other departments have priorities of their own. Service departments such as facilities or information technology, in particular, get many requests for help and they have to prioritize those requests. You can't expect everyone else to be in your rush—that is, be on your same time schedule or have the same sense of urgency as you do.

Most service departments have a process of submitting work orders. These allow them to track what's going on, prioritize requests by level of importance, and keep metrics on their workload and accomplishments. These metrics also give them a great deal of data from which they can estimate how long it reasonably takes to get certain tasks accomplished. Once they understand the nature of the problem they are being asked to fix, they can plan their time accordingly, along with any routine or scheduled tasks that are currently in place. Keep in mind, on the positive side, that because service or support departments are metrics-driven, once they open a work order or ticket, they don't want to keep it open any longer than necessary.

Let's look at your question from the point of view of expectations and communication. Someone in your department is experiencing a computer problem and wants it fixed now. If IT is on-site, rather than a remote help desk, the reasonable expectation could be that a technician will be in your department shortly. However, what if there is a problem with a database that affects an entire department and all available technicians are working on that right now? Today may be the day for a major system maintenance or upgrade project to which most of the IT staff is dedicated. The CEO's administrative assistant may have just called IT to solicit help for her or her boss's computer problem. Likely, that could delay getting to your request.

Has the problem been sufficiently explained to IT? Knowing the exact nature of the problem, IT can acknowledge the request, set up a work order, and provide a reasonable time frame in which they can resolve the problem for you or your team member. Realistically, the non-technical staff member may not know what the problem is, only that his computer isn't working. That can cause frustration for both sides. It may also be more time consuming to resolve because the problem will require some troubleshooting on IT's part.

Another dynamic often occurs with staff functions—reporting relationships. Consider who IT or facilities report to—often a senior executive. That can influence the priority of attention an issue will receive. There is a human tendency to want to please the boss before pleasing the customers.

The more you get to know your peers in other departments, the more you will learn about how other departments function within your organization. This will be a tremendous boost to managing expectations when you or one of your team members needs their support and assistance.

Question: I want to have a good relationship with human resources and wonder if there are some questions I should be asking as we work together.

Answer: Having a strong partnership with your HR leader is so important and great things can happen when you work together. HR can serve as a sounding board, conscience, coach, subject matter expert, and facilitator to help you handle your managerial duties.

One way to strengthen the relationship is to ask specific questions to jump-start a discussion that can greatly influence the organization's success.

Here are some questions to get you started:

- "What can I do to support you as you work to ensure we have the right people in place to meet our strategic goals?"

- "Is there a role you need me to play to support your efforts to hire, on-board, engage, and retain our talented workforce?"
- "Is there anything you think I could do better to be an effective manager?"
- "Do you have any suggestions for me on how I can communicate more effectively with my staff?"

If you start with these open-ended questions and listen carefully to the responses from HR, odds are your working relationship with HR will be on the right road.

If your HR leader has some ideas about how you can contribute, don't automatically dismiss them. For example, you may be asked to take an active role in your organization's college recruiting program. It is highly effective to have managers do class presentations and go on campus for recruiting events.

Another way HR may enlist your assistance is in the on-boarding process. There are many ways you can contribute to the increasingly important process of bringing new hires into your organizational culture. Some organizations, rather than having HR conduct the on-boarding process, ask department managers to present what their department does so that new hires get to know other managers and other functions.

When you have a strong partnership with your HR leader, consider using them as a coach to help you "up your game." Many HR leaders are great listeners and can help you make good decisions about your staff and any challenges you're facing.

It goes without saying that this is a two-way street. Hopefully, your HR leader will ask you what they can do to better support you and your efforts to be a good manager. Be honest and respectful when you ask for help or give them feedback.

Building this partnership requires trust and respect for what each brings. You both need to be able to truly listen to the other and to trust that anything that's said is kept confidential.

There's one last question you might consider asking and that is "What keeps you up at night?" You will learn a lot from the answers you get that should help you understand better the challenges HR faces. When we understand each other, we work better together!

Question: I'm new to management and I'm trying to increase my business literacy. I hear the term "operations" or "business operations" often. I have a sense of what it means in my organization. Can you provide me a clearer explanation?

Answer: The concept of business operations can be perplexing because it can mean different things in different organizations. Business operations focuses on getting goods and services to the organization's customers and clients. The basic concepts may be more relatable in organizations that produce goods, but the basics of operations also exist in service organizations. The concepts that drive operations and major considerations of those concepts include:

- **Capacity,** which is the organization's ability to yield output—its goods and services. Are there sufficient resources (supplies, equipment, and staff, for example) required for production of goods? Does the firm have sufficient staff, experience, and knowledge to provide the services for a client?
- **Standards,** which are measurements of the quality of output within the guidelines of certain requirements (for example, financial, time, or safety). Will we be able to produce the goods or services on time and on budget?
- **Scheduling,** which is the detailed planning process and coordination of resources, including their allocation. Scheduling draws upon current or incoming work, such as work orders or projects, history, and forecasts of future demand. Who are the best consultants to assign to new clients? If demand for our product increases, do we have the resources to meet that demand?
- **Inventory,** which is relevant to manufacturing, describes everything and anything that goes into the production process, such as supplies and raw materials; goods in various stages of production; and finished goods to

be shipped and sold. Can we move inventory at a rate at which we can see a return and don't incur carrying costs?

- **Control,** which is the evaluation of the organization's ability to meet both its own specifications and its customers' or clients' needs. Was the capacity there? Were resources used properly? Were all applicable standards met? The evaluation looks at what actually happened, compared it to what was supposed to happen, and determines what changes may need to be made for the future.

All of the above concepts are interrelated. Capacity utilization is dependent on scheduling. For example, in a services environment, there may be sufficient expertise on staff, but if they are engaged on current projects, they may not be available for new ones. Scheduling, in a manufacturing environment, is affected by inventory. If the supplies and raw materials aren't sufficiently available, production can't be scheduled.

Finally, although operations may be at the center of an organization, that doesn't mean that it exists in a vacuum. It is dependent on both external and internal partners. With the evolution of supply chain management, the management of the flow of goods and services, including the movement and storage of raw materials, of work-in-process inventory, and of finished goods from point of origin to point of consumption, organizations often forge strategic partnering relationships with their key suppliers who use technology to share information regarding the flow and movement of materials. Internally, operations is dependent on the integration of its organizations systems from accounting to warehouse operations to transportation.

Question: I've heard the terms "reverse mentoring" and "peer mentoring." Is there any difference between these terms, and do they have any advantages in the workplace?

Answer: Mentoring in the traditional sense occurs when someone who is older and more experienced works with younger employees to support the younger employee's professional growth and development. The more experienced individual (in the workplace) was providing guidance to someone with less workplace experience.

The concept of reverse mentoring pairs older workers with younger ones so they can educate each other. The early focus of reverse mentoring was on younger workers helping their older peers and even executives with technology issues. Millennials, the generation of workers born roughly between the years 1981 and 1997, grew up with technology and are very tech-savvy. Using technology is second nature for them and it's easier for them to adapt to new technology than their older peers and managers.

As members of different generations are paired, some interesting outgrowths occur. Relationships form and the peers start educating each other on how business works and on new ways of thinking—how improvements can be made. It gives both parties the opportunity to see things through a different set of lenses. It becomes peers mentoring each other, whether formally or informally, and it usually happens organically—thus, peer mentoring.

There certainly are positive aspects of these relationships. As generations get to know more about each other, this can negate many of the negative stereotypes that are often associated with Millennial workers, such as that they are lazy, entitled, or are easily distracted by technology. Giving Millennials these opportunities addresses their desire to contribute in meaningful ways. They want to share what they know. It keeps them engaged. Reverse mentoring can also enhance an organization's diversity efforts by bringing together people from different generations and backgrounds. It can also bring people from different parts or levels within the organization together, broadening diversity efforts.

Closing the knowledge gap in organizations can be achieved, at least in part, with reverse mentoring. Older workers can possess a great deal of institutional knowledge as well as business knowledge that they can share with younger workers. Younger workers can learn much about business terminology and industry practices from their older peers. With technology changing at lightning speed, younger peers grasp these changes quickly and are positioned to share, saving time and money.

Reverse mentoring can also play a part in career development and in developing leaders. Older peers can often introduce younger ones to their networks both inside and outside the organization. Conversely, younger peers can share their virtual networks and explain how they work to their older peers. This can raise the professional profile of both groups. When younger workers have access to leaders in their organization, it is the first step in preparing them to become the next generation of leaders. Having the freedom to interact with leaders gives them the opportunity to observe first-hand leadership in action.

As a manager, encourage your staff to engage in peer mentoring. It's a good way to keep life-long learning alive in your organization!

Question: I'm having difficulty working with my manager. Do you have some ideas for how to develop that relationship so we can work better together?

Answer: You've hit on something that is sometimes known as "managing up." This is a method of career development that's based on consciously working for the mutual benefit of your manager and you. It's all about understanding your boss's position, goals, and responsibilities and working to always exceeds expectations—especially when what you do helps your manager achieve one of her goals.

Let's be clear that managing up is not about "kissing up to the boss"! Yes, you certainly want to please your manager, but the best way to do that is to accomplish all your job requirements in an efficient and excellent manner so that you're making the maximum contribution possible. Your contributions to the success of your department will make your manager look good and, hopefully, be grateful for your assistance.

Here are some easy dos and don'ts to successfully manage up:

- Do begin by getting to know your manager by observation and by conversations you have during your one-on-one sessions or in staff meetings. You want to know:
  — What are her priorities?
  — What does she value professionally and personally?
  — How does she communicate and how does she want you to communicate with her?
  — What role does she see you taking in the department?

- Do always be helpful. Volunteer for special projects and team assignments that you know will factor into one of your department's deliverables. If there is a routine task your manager doesn't enjoy doing like creating PowerPoint presentations and you like that kind of work, why not make the offer to either work with your manager or take it on yourself? You could be a hero and have a golden opportunity to work one-one-one with your boss and get to know her better!
- Do what you say you will do. By keeping commitments in a timely manner, your manager will learn to trust you and may encourage you to take on new responsibilities.
- Do look for ways you can help your manager out in crisis situations. Let's say a very last-minute request comes down to your manager from the CEO for a report needed for a board meeting and you know your manager isn't great at pulling data together. Make the offer to take on part of the job and let your manager do what she's best at.
- Don't be the "yes person" in meetings. Be honest and friendly with your manager and your team members so that you're seen as a valued resource to your manager and others. Stay out of office politics by staying professional at all times. Treat everyone with respect, including your manager!

Having a good working relationship with your manager also should make your job more enjoyable!

Question: I find myself in a situation in which I need to exert influence on my peers, but I certainly don't have the authority to make them follow my lead. What can I do?

Answer: This is a challenge most of us face at one time or another in our careers. It's challenging but certainly not impossible. Here are some things you may want to consider:

- It's easier to influence other people if they like you. That may sound simplistic and not very businesslike, but it's the truth! Think about your own reaction to people you work with. Aren't you more likely to go along with the likeable ones? We're not suggesting you change your personality but try to be friendly and kind to others so that you can build personal relationships with your peers. This means keeping your promises and not undermining the work of others to get your way. Show your authentic self at work!

- Do your best to understand the people you need to influence. Observe them in meetings and social situations, and see if you can figure out what motivates them. You may discover that, though someone appears to be negative, they just don't want to be the first to try something new. They like to wait until they see how it goes and then get on board or not, depending on what's the safest course of action.

- When you know what motivates your peers, look for a way to make your idea work for them. Remember the "What's in it for me?" maxim and see if you can tailor your presentation so that each person sees how it will impact them in a positive manner.

- Is there anyone who you think agrees with you on this issue? It's always a good strategy to find others who agree with your position before you present your idea to everyone. Line up support beforehand and your chances of success will increase.

- Be sure to do your homework before attempting to influence people you don't have authority over. If you have solid facts and figures to back up your idea, your chances of success increase. Get your facts lined up and be sure to do a cost/benefit analysis so that you can show how your idea will make a positive difference in your organization.

- Remember that "every how needs a why," and the stronger you can make the case for why your idea will benefit your organization, the easier your influencing job may be.

- When you present your idea, take time to listen to the objections of your peers—really listen before you jump in with why you're right and they're wrong. You may need to compromise to move forward, so listening to what others think can make the difference in your idea becoming reality!

- Don't give up if you really believe in something. It may take some time to win over others, but keep trying.

Question: I feel as if I one of my roles as a manager is to protect my employees so that they can focus on their work. I'm just not sure how far that goes. Can you give me some tips?

Answer: You're right. One of the roles a manager plays is to shield your staffers from distractions and to run interference, if needed, when organizational politics come into play.

Start by getting to know each person you manage well enough to know when your help will be needed. For example, you may be able to spot a time when they're worried about something but they're not comfortable in asking you for help. If you take some of the burden off their shoulders or work alongside them on a project, you're providing something quite valuable to your employees.

You definitely want to encourage a climate of safety and comfort for your employees. If your employees feel as if you have their back, they will be much more inclined to admit mistakes or come to you when they need your help.

Unfortunately, there will be circumstances when you can't protect your people, including layoffs or pay cuts due to organizational cutbacks, but you can be compassionate and try to blunt negative consequences when things are beyond your control.

Serving as a buffer isn't comfortable for some managers, but it is a role that is highly valued by your employees. If it doesn't come naturally to you, here are some ways you can support your staff:

- **Protect their time.** When one of your employees has a deadline to complete a project, you can step up and take less critical work off their to-do list. Maybe you can assign some work to others or move a deadline back on the less-critical work to allow your employee to concentrate.

- **Run interference.** When your CEO is on a rampage and lashes out against one of your team, you should step in and take the heat. This is not to say if your employee is in the wrong, you let them get away with it. It means you put yourself between the higher-up and your employee and then you handle the required disciplinary action.
- **Create a space in which it is okay to make mistakes.** People need to know how they will be treated if they make a mistake. Your employees learn best from actually doing the work, but they may not be perfect the first time they tackle a challenging assignment. If they know that you are there for them to answer questions and you will support them, most people will do their best to not let you down.
- **Take the heat if a mistake is made.** This is the ultimate in buffering when you don't throw your employee under the bus but instead admit to the mistake.

Creating the comfortable atmosphere your employees crave takes some effort on your part, but it is well worth it, and they'll want to protect you, too.

Question: I want to set clear boundaries so that we have a more efficient and pleasant working atmosphere. I need some help. Can you advise me how to get started?

Answer: Setting boundaries as soon as possible in any working relationship will help establish your role as manager and will clarify your expectations on how things will operate in your department or business. Clear boundaries help people be more productive as well as happier and healthier at work.

Some managers don't think it's necessary to discuss boundaries at work. They think that by the time people enter the workforce, they should know how to behave at work, but that's just not the case. We all can use a reminder from time to time.

Setting workplace boundaries is not coming up with hard and fast rules for what people can and can't do; rather, it is a way to get things out in the open and to discuss how we want to work together. Your goal is to have a professional work environment in which everyone is valued and is encouraged to do their best work at all times.

Not having clear boundaries can have a real impact on your staff and on your productivity. Morale can suffer as people cross lines at work. Unclear boundaries can also de-motivate your staff if they feel as if their contributions aren't valued.

And here's where unclear boundaries can really cause your organization major difficulties: If an employee disrespects another employee, it can lead to harassment and even to legal action.

So, setting clear boundaries for how you work together is an imperative for good management.

Hopefully, your organization has a values component to your mission statement that says "Employees are treated with dignity and respect" or something like that. This is a great place to begin your boundaries discussion with your staff.

Don't worry if your organization doesn't have a values statement. You can fill that gap by creating one for your department. Here's a sample to consider: "The XYZ Department values the contributions of every employee and treats each person with respect so that we maintain a civil and professional work environment."

Once you have your values statement, start to add the guiding principles—behaviors you want to see exhibited in your workplace. Here are some to consider:

- We will work to build positive relationships with peers.
- We will show respect for others at all times.
- We will work efficiently with others.
- We will celebrate the successes of others.
- We will listen with respect to our coworkers.
- We will show concern for others.
- We will show professional courtesy to others.
- We will listen to others with undivided attention.

Taking the time to set boundaries will be extremely helpful as you work to be an effective manager. If this is new to you, consider asking other managers for their ideas or ask for help from HR to facilitate the discussion to create your department's boundaries.

Question: I want to be sure we're providing our customers with the best possible service, but I keep hearing that good service isn't enough—that we have to give them a good customer experience. How can I make sure we are doing that?

Answer: Usually, your customer's first contact with your organization is through an interaction with one of your employees, either in person or on the phone. That's customer service. If a customer calls your restaurant for a reservation for a special occasion at a time that is already booked but your employee finds them a table, that's customer experience.

Customer experience goes beyond service and is defined by interactions between a customer and organization throughout their business relationship. Customer expectations are higher than ever and word of mouth travels fast—especially in our highly connected world.

Here's why this matters. A customer who has a positive experience with your organization or business is more likely to become a repeat and loyal customer and refer friends and family to your organization. In its simplest terms, happy customers remain loyal.

Here are some ideas to try:

- **Create an emotional connection with your customers,** because customers become loyal when they remember how they felt when they used a particular service or product. Studies show that an emotionally engaged customer is at least three times more likely to recommend your product or service.[1] Emotional connections are formed when your employee finds a way to do something so special for a customer that the person is blown away. Consider this example from Zappos where a customer returned a pair of shoes she'd bought for her mother who died before she could wear them. Not only did the customer service representative have the shoes picked up by a courier service at no cost to the customer, they also sent flowers with a condolence note to the customer.[2] You can bet that customer is loyal to Zappos!

- **Ask for feedback from your customers and do it
  quickly.** Have you noticed how quickly you get a survey
  from places where you shop or visit? Sometimes you've
  barely returned home before a survey pops up on your
  email. That's because those organizations have learned
  the value of collecting data in real time. What you do
  with the data is critical. Be sure it gets to a specific customer support person so they can learn.
- **Ask for feedback from your customer service staff.**
  They are the ones on the front lines, and they may have
  valuable information you can use to improve your product or service. Including your front-line staff also is a
  huge morale booster for them—especially when you act
  on their suggestions, so let them know when you make
  changes based on their feedback.

There is one simple question you can ask to evaluate how your
customers view their experiences with you: "Would you recommend
this organization to a friend or relative?" Try this and see what you
learn. If necessary, modify your customer service processes.

Closing Thoughts

It takes more than diplomacy to impact people outside your scope
of authority—peers or your manager—or to manage external business partners. You have to take the time to learn and understand how
things are done and the contributions that others make to your team
and to the organization. Armed with this knowledge, you can perfect
your skills. You are positioning yourself to be a skilled influencer in
your organization.

Avoiding Potential Land Mines

You've learned that management is not always black and white. Some situations are tenuous (like workplace violence or delivering bad news); others are more complicated than they need to be (like having fun at work). Barriers appear to be in the way (like the need for background checks or reporting and record-keeping requirements). The questions and answers in this section shed light on these and other situations that could trip up even an experienced manager.

Question: One of my employees constantly pleads with me to intervene on her behalf. She has good ideas about process improvement, yet her team leader is unbending. On one hand I want to intervene because of her good ideas, but I don't want to appear to be taking sides, nor demotivate the team leader. Both are valued employees and I want to keep them engaged. What can I do to resolve this disagreement?

Answer: Managers often find themselves trapped in the middle of a situation involving employees—situations or issues that are not theirs to solve. You've recognized the dilemma in this tense circumstance. Here are some things you can do to foster a collaborative work environment:

- **Give your employees the space to grow.** They need the freedom and authority to solve problems that relate to their work. Provide the opportunity for them to learn conflict-management techniques and develop problem-solving skills. Learn as much as possible about conflict management and model the techniques and skills you learn.

- **Recognize that tension, egos, and emotions often get in the way.** Help develop good working relationships among team members. Define the problem and the impact it's having in the workplace. Don't discount emotions—they are often the person's passion around an issue. If emotions flare, help the employees control and balance them by calling for a break to give everyone the time to reflect. It's an opportunity to regain balance so discussions can continue in a constructive way.

- **Strengthen your own facilitation skills.** As a manager, you're often a neutral observer to a conflict. This is a great vantage point from which you can guide employees through a mediated discussion. When you meet with them, define roles and set ground rules. The employees are the primary players, not you. They are the ones who'll be asking questions of each other and proposing solutions. You won't offer advice, opinions, or solutions, even if asked. You're there to keep the discussion on track.

- **Optimize conflict.** Conflict is often creativity and innovation trying to happen. Employees close to the work often have great ideas for better solutions. Help them brainstorm, then evaluate and prioritize these ideas. When people sit down and talk calmly and rationally, information is exchanged. It is an opportunity to hear and understand different viewpoints and strengthen working relationships. Embrace the point of view that conflict is essential in the workplace if it's part of a creative and engaged culture that wants the organization to grow and thrive.

Question: I often get phone calls from service providers and outside vendors, such as staffing companies, or supply and equipment providers, who would like to meet with me often suggesting we do so over lunch. I've been hesitant to accept. Is there any reason why I shouldn't take them up on these offers to meet?

Answer: You're right to exercise caution. It may be tempting to accept an invitation for a nice lunch, but you'd be wise to check with your colleagues in other departments to make sure there are no restrictions that prohibit accepting meals and gifts from service providers and vendors, or existing contracts already in place.

Ask about existing policies and protocols. Human resources, for example, will typically have processes in place for conducting searches for candidates and selecting the best ones. These are driven by best practices and government regulations. It would be helpful for you to not only understand what they are, but also why they are in place. Should you meet with a staffing agency and they present a candidate to you outside of the organization's process—and this could be as simple as their sending you a resume—you could be liable for a placement fee for that candidate should you hire them, even at a future date. There are also record-keeping, and possibly affirmative action, requirements regarding the hiring process, and you could risk violating them.

There may be limited budgets around these goods and services of which you are not aware, so it would be a good idea to check with finance. When contracts are negotiated, organizations look to maximize their buying power, especially if they plan to spend a large amount of money. Whereas you may be considering a decision based on your department's needs, other staff departments (such as purchasing, finance, HR, IT, and legal) are looking at the needs of the entire organization.

Also, if your organization has an existing contract for the goods or services that these sales reps are calling about, there may be restrictions or other conditions in those contracts. For example, there may be a contract clause stating that a certain provider has exclusive rights, meaning your organization can't do business with another firm.

Rebates may have been negotiated, meaning that once a certain level of sales has been reached, the provider will return a certain percentage to you or provide a credit against future sales. You don't want to risk inadvertently violating one of the terms of a contract. Contracts can be complicated. That's why the legal team gets involved in negotiations and review.

Keep in mind that representatives from other organizations may have more interest in making a sale than they are in understanding your organization's processes and requirements. If that's the case, they are probably not a good cultural fit. They also may assume that because you have agreed to meet with them, you have the authority to represent your organization, which you may or may not have. Make sure that if you do meet, you are clear that the purpose of the meeting is to gather information. Consider inviting a colleague—perhaps someone from another staff department—to join the meeting. This will provide another set of ears from a different vantage point.

Question: It seems like we can't have fun at work anymore with concerns about diversity, harassment, and other sensitivities. What can I do to lighten the mood when things are stressful without crossing any lines?

Answer: Indeed, levity in the workplace can help break the stress and have a positive impact on productivity. Lightening up can help your organization be more profitable.

However, trouble can lurk when fun is had at someone else's expense. That's when issues such as harassment, bias, and potential bullying can enter the workplace, and they are not fun to address. When the nature of jokes and comments becomes sexually suggestive or racially or ethnically pointed, for example, or when jokes or comments are made about another person or their characteristics, that's when lines are crossed and disruptive (or illegal) behavior encroaches.

Many highly successful companies have incorporated fun and lightheartedness into their workplaces. Playing games and engaging in activities also stimulate creativity. The following are examples of things that you can do, many of which are no cost or low cost:

- Theme days where employees can dress to a certain theme (e.g., retro day dressing from a certain era or Western day). Employees can also decorate their workspace according to the theme and compete for prizes.
- Trivia events (during breaks, lunch, etc.) that includes trivia questions about the organization's history, products, highlights, and so forth.
- Game days, when games can be set up in break rooms, or in places around the offices, or at off-site meetings. This can include board games, card games, video games, miniature golf, or similar activities.
- Staff meetings with ice-breaker activities such as everyone tells two truths and one lie about themselves and others have to guess which one the lie is.
- Improv comedy sessions and have everyone participate.
- Celebrations for meeting deadlines with pizza, ice cream socials, or some other type of reward.
- Potlucks, chili cookoffs, best cookie contests, or tailgate parties in the parking lot.

The list of things you can do is endless, but be respectful of boundaries. For example, if you engage in games or cooking contests, be sure that all your team members are comfortable with these activities. Be sure that as a manager, you participate and encourage the members of the senior management team to do so as well. This is important because it shows a different side of them from what employees usually experience.

Question: I referred a great candidate for my team. She's someone I worked with in the past. My manager and other team members have interviewed her, but human resources says background checks have to be done before we can offer her a job. How can I change their mind?

Answer: It's good that you want to get this great candidate hired! It may seem as if human resources is a bottleneck in the process, but there are good reasons for doing references and conducting background checks.

Organizations can be liable for claims of negligent hiring or negligent retention. Negligent hiring means that if someone is injured by an employee who has been careless or committed some wrong on the job, the injured person—another employee, a client, or a customer—can claim that it's the organization's fault because they put that employee in a situation where they hurt them. Employers are generally responsible for their employees' behaviors when the employees are performing their jobs. In negligent hiring claims, the employer is responsible when the employee is acting outside the scope of their job duties and commits an egregious act that harms someone else. In that case, the injured person can claim the employer should have known—and would have known had a background check been conducted—the person presented a risk, and could have taken steps to prevent it, such as declining to hire the person.

Negligent retention claims occur when an employer fails to be aware of a current employee's unfitness for their position and therefore fails to take any corrective action such as reassignment or discharge to remedy the problem. Negligent hiring occurs during the recruitment and offer phase of employment and is a failure of the employer to adequately investigate an applicant's background. Negligent retention occurs during the course of the employment when the employer fails to investigate or otherwise act upon an employee's potential unfitness to do their current job.

Although you can probably provide a good reference for the candidate in your question, it's important that human resources follow the same process for all potential employees. This ensures that everyone is treated fairly. It also ensures the integrity of the process in the event the hiring decision should ever be questioned.

Question: At times, a manager has to deliver bad news. The most common circumstance is having to terminate an employee. With concerns about social media and public relations, how can I avoid negative backlash in these situations?

Answer: You are right to be concerned. Organizations often find themselves in difficult public relations positions, and many times the situations leading up to negative press could have been avoided. Even if organizations—and their managers in particular—do everything right, there is still no guarantee that there will be no subsequent backlash, especially on social media. Unfortunately, people turn to social media to vent and they are often lacking the facts. Nevertheless, there are some things you can and should do to handle tenuous situations with diplomacy and care.

Whenever you have to deliver bad news, particularly news of a termination, it's important to convey dignity and respect for the individual. Always deliver the news in person to the extent possible. Of course, if the employee works in a distant geographic location, the next best thing would be a personal phone call. Never, under any circumstances, should you deliver news of a termination via email. In the rare situation where you have been unable to contact the person by phone, then send a certified letter to them.

If the termination is occurring for cause—the employee has received disciplinary actions or a plan for performance improvement—then the news should not take the employee by surprise. They should be expecting the termination because you, as a manager, have communicated that there has been a problem.

In some circumstances, however, an involuntary termination may be the result of a reduction in force—a layoff—and the affected employees may, in fact, be caught off guard. In these circumstances, senior management, including any internal or external legal, human resources, and communications team, have likely put a plan in place to handle all aspects of the layoff and you should be coordinating with them.

Whatever the circumstances for the termination, written notification should be delivered to the employee when you sit down to deliver the news. That notification should explain the reason behind the termination. When people are given bad news in a personal way it gives them the opportunity to ask questions and receive clarification. This can diffuse any ill feelings and avoid any unintended risk, such as the individual telling their story to the local press and saying things they otherwise might not have said.

In the case of layoffs, give as much notice as possible. Overcommunicate and be open and honest to all employees, even those who will not be affected. Remember that they are losing their colleagues and may be asked to take on additional work. Keep in mind there are sites like Glass Door where employees can post negative information about organizations. If they witness that their colleagues were treated with respect and dignity, it will help morale, and they will likely work harder and refrain from posting negative comments online. In fact, they are likely to post positive ones instead.

Question: I've always worked for small organizations where getting things done was easy and flexible. I recently joined a large company in a different industry, and there are so many requirements around getting authorizations and keeping records. Can you shed some light on why all of these rules are in place?

Answer: It can be frustrating when you're working in a different environment, especially when things appear to be more complex than you are used to them being. There can be many reasons why you're seeing so many requirements.

Different organizations in different industries can be subject to oversight by a number of governmental agencies. Depending on size, different laws and regulations apply. For example, at the federal level, most organizations, except very small ones, are subject to regulations by the Department of Labor. If the organization provides goods and services to the federal government, additional requirements are added. Publicly traded companies must comply with Securities and Exchange Commission regulations, and organizations in the communications industry must comply with the Federal Communications Commission's regulations.

In many organizations accurate reporting of hours worked is essential to their operations. This data often forms the basis for pricing or for billing customers. Timekeeping practices are often subject to audit by the Department of Labor and other agencies, depending on the industry.

In addition to timesheet reporting, other records are prepared such as financial reports, accounting records, business plans, environmental reports, injury and accident reports, and expense reports, to name a few. Many individuals and entities, both within and outside the organization, may depend upon these reports to be accurate and truthful for a variety of reasons. These people and entities include, but are not limited to, the employees, governmental agencies, auditors, and the communities in which the organization operates. In addition, honest and accurate recording and reporting of information helps the organization to make responsible business decisions.

It's not that unusual in larger organizations to require prior authorization before certain things can happen. For example, purchase requisitions are required before equipment or supplies can be bought or personnel requisitions before staff can be hired. In some industries, prior authorization for travel is required. It's not only a way to let management know what's going on, but it also assures conformance to established standards and, in some cases, government regulations.

Don't hesitate to confer with the appropriate support staff in your organization (human resources, finance, purchasing, legal, or others). They will be happy to provide you with guidance and explain why these requirements exist. This will assure you don't inadvertently breach a policy or procedure that's in place.

Question: There seems to be so many internal reporting requirements in my new organization. Is it overkill or are there reasons for it?

Answer: In most organization managers are expected to resolve many issues. However, there are other issues that are better handled by the staff who are more experienced with them, generally human resources and legal. Here are some of those issues:

- **Discrimination or harassment complaints,** even if the employee requests that the issue be kept confidential. It should be reported because the organization, once it has notice of the issue, must investigate it and take appropriate corrective action.
- **Allegations of criminal or fraudulent activities** that may be in violation of statutes such as the Sarbanes-Oxley Act. In addition, alleged violations of the organization's policies that may have legal or business consequences such as conflict of interest. This is important because a judge or a jury may view failure to report complaints of this nature as perpetuating any wrongdoing.

- **Disclosure by an employee or applicant of medical information or condition** should be referred to your human resources or legal support, because it could be a request, albeit an indirect one, for a reasonable accommodation under the Americans With Disabilities Act (ADA). Human resources and legal are more knowledgeable about the ADA's requirements and the process of making accommodations.

- **Requests for leaves of absence** should also be referred to your human resources or legal support because the leave could be covered under the Family & Medical Leave Act (FMLA), and they are more knowledgeable and experienced with the requirements.

- **Work-related accidents and injuries** should also be reported to your human resources support because there are certain reporting and record-keeping requirements under the Occupational Safety and Health Act (OSHA). In addition, on-the-job injuries entitle employees to benefits under workers' compensation.

- **Evidence of union activity** should be reported to your human resources or legal support as soon as possible. Early detection of and rapid response to union activity has long been key to union avoidance.

- **Communications from government agencies** should be reported to your human resources or legal support as soon as you receive it. This is important because the manner in which the employer communicates can determine the legal outcome and any damages that may flow from it.

- **Communications from outside attorneys** should be reported immediately to your legal support team. This includes subpoenas or other legal documents, letters from lawyers who do not represent your organization, and even "friendly" calls from lawyers who are "just curious" about a few things.

- **Threats or signs of violence** should be reported to your human resources or security support. They are better equipped to handle these situations and have ready access to external resources that can assist such as an Employee Assistance Program (EAP) professional or law enforcement in extreme circumstances.

Reporting issues such as these to the appropriate staff assures that issues are allocated to those individuals with the appropriate knowledge, skills, and experience and they will handle them in an appropriate manner that best helps the organization and mitigates the risk. It also frees up a manager's time to focus on your own responsibilities and the operation of your department.

Question: I now manage several people who work remotely, and this is a new challenge for me. Do you have any suggestions on how I can maximize their effectiveness?

Answer: It's a challenge to effectively manage people you don't see every day but telecommuting is a fact of life and it just takes doing some things differently. There are many configurations of a remote relationship. You may have staff that works in different time zones or even on different continents, or perhaps they work from home several days a week.

Hopefully your organization has a well-crafted policy for remote workers. It should be your guideline and help you accurately measure productivity. The policy should also assist the virtual worker to deal with some of the issues they face, such as how to stay visible and vital in an organization where they aren't seen in person.

You do need to manage your remote employees differently, and this takes some thought and extra effort on your part. You are held responsible for the work your employees produce, be they in the office or working in another state or country. Here are some suggestions for partnering with your remote employees to maximize their effectiveness:

- **Set expectations.** Be sure your remote employees (and all your employees for that matter) know exactly what you expect from them and when. Let them know how you will measure success against your expectations and give them a chance to ask for clarity. It wouldn't hurt to put your expectations in writing so that there's no room for doubt.

- **Hold employees accountable.** Whether your employees are in your location or halfway around the world, follow up with your employees to ensure they're on track. Set milestones to ensure what you are expecting to be accomplished will be done to your expectations. There is a fine line here where you don't want to micromanage. Remember that you are the one who is ultimately responsible for the work, so hold your employees accountable for their part in the process.

- **Be available.** Have regularly scheduled meeting times set with your virtual staff but also do your best to be available when they need you. This can be difficult due to time differences but if you set the expectation that you will respond to emails, texts, and calls in a specific time period, your remote staff will feel more comfortable.

- **Communicate.** Be sure that they receive (and are aware of) other important organizational communications. Make sure other team members are in contact with them as well.

- **Use technology.** None of this would be possible if it wasn't for technology, and you should make use of every possible tool at your fingertips. It's possible to hold staff meetings at which virtual employees can actively participate—including doing breakout sessions and whiteboarding exercises. Skype, Zoom, and Facetime allow you to "see" each other as often as you probably see the people down the hall!

- **Recognize and reward.** Don't overlook your remote staff when handing out compliments and/or prizes. Treat everyone of your staff the same—in the office or not!

Remote workers are increasingly important in today's organizations. Yes, they present challenges, but they can help your department be highly productive if managed appropriately.

Question: I just joined an organization that has a telecommuting policy and I've never managed telecommuters before. Most of the positions in our department are suitable for telecommuting, but I'm concerned about determining which employees will make the best candidates. What should I consider as I review requests for telecommuting?

Answer: Today's employees crave flexibility, and with advances in technology, telecommuting is probably a trend that is here to stay. Organizations take different approaches to it. Employees may work a day or two a week from home, or they may work from home the majority of the time and come into the office periodically for meetings.

It sounds as if many of the positions your employees hold are compatible with the telecommuting policy—that is, the nature of the work is independent and/or it requires a great deal of concentration. If that's the case, consider allowing employees to work from home on an intermittent basis (one or two days a week) and vary their schedules so that not everyone is out on the same days. You may also want to rotate their days off. In some geographic areas, traffic is heaviest in the middle of the week and allowing everyone to periodically have the chance to work from home on Tuesdays and Wednesdays to avoid the stress of traffic could be a real plus.

If your employees are looking for more permanent telecommuting arrangements, consider the following in choosing the candidates: their self-motivation, performance, organization and time-management skills, and familiarity with the job and work. Their tenure with the organization, though an important consideration, should not be the overriding factor.

Many of the management challenges for teleworkers are the same as for remote workers (those individuals who work in different geographic locations). You've got to be sure to set expectations and hold them accountable. You've also got to be available for them and communicate on a regular basis. Getting telecommuters into the office for periodic meetings is easier than for remote workers. You may want to consider having them regularly work in the office one or two days a month so they remain visible. This is important, because there are a number of challenges for the telecommuting employee as well. They include:

- **Isolation and lack of interaction.** Teleworkers may perceive that they lack the ability to collaborate with team members. With today's technology, much of this can be alleviated, but be sure you have regular check-in meetings.
- **Household distractions.** These can be bigger issues for employees on a deadline. Sometimes having the ability to get away from work for a few minutes to tend to something else can be a welcome distraction that helps the employee refocus.
- **Lack of support services.** These can be addressed through portals to the organization's internal services.
- **Hindrance to career advancement opportunities.** It's important to provide training to all employees about career management, but for teleworkers it can be more critical. Good communication vehicles and regular time in the office can help mitigate the perception that a telecommuter's career could suffer.

Be sure that any employee who telecommutes on a regular basis is aware of these challenges. Communicate with them frequently about how they are managing them and lend your support. Telecommuting has many advantages for the employees, the organization, and the community.

Question: Generational issues and differences seem to be big in the workplace today, and I'm certainly noticing them in mine. How can I better understand and manage them?

Answer: People are different and individuals are unique, but common experiences shape a generation's thinking and cause them to bring different perspectives to the workplace. Bridging this generation gap at work happens by recognizing that we are all at different stages of our lives and possess different career aspirations and needs. As with any diversity challenge, figuring out what's unique brings about greater understanding and a recognition that we have more in common than we realize.

A difficult difference that older managers and employees have to adapt to is that the younger generations don't view work in the same way as they did. Work, for the younger generations, is not the main focus of their life and/or their identity. Moreover, as they've watched their parents and older friends and relatives go through layoffs and downsizings, they don't see that loyalty to an organization pays off. They are more inclined to want to have a life outside of work that is meaningful. So do the older generations, but the younger ones seem to be better at making it happen.

Younger workers were raised with technology, making them would-be experts on everything technical. They were the CIOs of their neighborhoods, so is it any wonder they assume they know how to do everything? They feel as if technology gives them a real edge in the workplace, and they know how to maximize its effectiveness to get work done in a shorter period of time. Why, they wonder, if their work is finished should they have to stay around the office? They don't understand why putting in long hours proves your dedication. After all, if results have been produced, does it really matter when the work gets done?

Younger workers also want meaningful work and the opportunity to make a contribution. They don't want to sit around and wait for that chance to make a contribution: They want to do it sooner rather than later. In today's competitive work environment, that's not a bad trait to have. Rather than try to mold younger generations' behaviors and habits to conform with workplaces of the past—workplaces that worked in a more industrial era—give them some flexibility to help shape the workplaces of the future—ones in which they will likely spend more time than their older counterparts.

A friendly environment, the ability to use their skills while learning something new, respect, the opportunity to help others, adequate paid time off and flexibility, health and welfare benefits, and the opportunity to do meaningful work—these are some of the things that younger workers are asking for. These are many of the things older workers wanted, but they just didn't know they could ask for them!

Working with multiple generations isn't impossible if you take the time to look for the common ground. Where there are differences, honor and respect them. Don't let these differences drive a wedge among coworkers.

Question: I manage a team of Millennial employees, and I want to maximize my effectiveness in leading this team of younger workers. Can you help me understand more about the traits they bring to the workplace?

Answer: Because Millennials are now the largest generation in the workplace, we all need to know as much as possible about their strengths and what they bring to the world of work. There have been so many negatives written about this large group of people, and much of it has been unfair. Let's look at what they value and how what they value is making a difference in our world of work:

- **Workplace Flexibility:** Most Millennials want to have the ability to work at their own pace and at a time that fits their personal life. They rebel against the traditional 9-to-5 workday. Technology allows anyone to work from anywhere at any time, so they aren't sure going to an office at a specific time and staying there until it's time to go makes sense. Why not work when you're at your personal best—even if that is in the middle of the night? Savvy organizations are finding ways to have more flexibility in hours and where work is done. There are some financial benefits to this in things like reduced real estate investments because so many people now work from home or telecommute a few days a week.

- **Feedback:** By asking or maybe even demanding more frequent feedback, Millennials have revolutionized how many organizations manage performance. This generation wants feedback as often as possible, so many

organizations have eliminated the annual performance
review and now do frequent check-ins with staff.

- **Collaboration:** This generation has been on teams
  from an early age and enjoys collaborating with others. This trait has had a positive impact on teams and on
  productivity.
- **Meaningful Work:** Millennials don't have to work for
  "name" organizations, but they want to work where
  what they do has meaning. It is important for them to
  know where their work fits into the strategic goals of
  their organization. Many do want to work for non-profits to improve the world, but they are also encouraging
  private sector employers to be more charitable.
- **Skill Development:** Millennials are totally committed to
  learning and growing, and are willing to devote personal
  time to gaining new skills. Smart employers understand
  that if this generation doesn't feel as if they are learning
  something new, they're not opposed to changing jobs to
  get it.
- **Productivity:** Millennials have no patience for doing
  things "the way we've always done them" if there's a better way to accomplish the same task. They are willing to
  try new things and take risks.

So, let's learn from Millennials because we don't see anything in
the preceding list that isn't good for our organizations or our people.
Many people of other generations now wish they'd been more open
with their employers so that they could have changed the world of
work in the positive ways Millennials are doing today.

**Question: I have an employee whose behavior has gotten very
volatile recently and I'm concerned. I want to address this behavior and offer some help through our Employee Assistance Program
(EAP), but I'm not sure where to begin. Any suggestions?**

Answer: It's good that you recognize this change in your employee's behavior and want to offer help. The EAP can often stabilize a

situation before it grows worse. Making a referral to the EAP for any reason can sometimes be difficult for a manager. When the situation is serious, such as erratic or volatile behavior, it is critical that it's done quickly. You should seek guidance from an EAP counselor who can help you assess the situation and prepare you to handle the situation so that the outcome is positive for both the employee and the organization.

In describing the behavior—to both the EAP counselor and the employee—be specific about the behavior that is causing concern. Provide the employee explicit, quantifiable facts that are hard to refute. For example, "On Monday, you yelled at your coworker in a tone of voice that was threatening. Several coworkers witnessed and reported it." This helps to break through the employee's denial that a problem exists. It also lets the employee know that you have noticed something and written it down.

When confronting the employee, keep in mind that you are not a counselor or healthcare provider. Avoid diagnosing the root of the problem. Leave this to the professionals. Your job is to focus on maintaining proficiency and productivity of your department.

During your discussion with the employee:

- Let the employee know what is expected: specific actions and a time frame for completion, including dates for follow-up.
- Document what has been communicated to the employee.
- Communicate that you will continue monitoring the employee and that absent improvement further action will be taken, specifying the action that could take place (e.g., termination).
- Initiate any parallel management action, such as a plan for performance improvement.
- Make a management referral to the Employee Assistance Program. Communicate that contacting the EAP is part of the action plan for improving the situation.

- Emphasize that the management referral is voluntary and that the EAP is offered as a resource to help. It's the employee's decision to take advantage of the help, but they will not be disciplined for failure to follow through on a management referral.
- Stress that The EAP is not a safe harbor. The employee remains accountable for their performance and behavior.

Remember that a management referral to the EAP is voluntary.

- No punitive action can result if the employee fails to contact the EAP (e.g., "If you don't call the EAP, you will be terminated.").
- No conditions can be placed on the referral (e.g., "I suggest you call the EAP by next Thursday.").

You will likely receive confirmation that the employee has or has not contacted the EAP, but you may or may not receive feedback regarding the employee's progress. That depends on whether the employee authorizes the counselor to contact you. Nevertheless, once the referral has been made, continue to observe, monitor, evaluate, and document the employee's performance. If there is no improvement, then further management action should be taken in accordance with your organization's policies.

Question: With the increase in violence in the workplace and society, are there any things in particular that I should be aware of as a manager?

Answer: Violence is a gruesome, disturbing reality today, and it's commendable that you are aware and want to be proactive. Prevention is the best defense against workplace violence, and your organization should have programs and plans in place such as management training, a response plan, and an Employee Assistance Program (EAP).

Managers play a crucial role in recognizing and addressing inappropriate workplace behavior. Intervening is the first line of defense for preventing potential violent incidents.

Some of signs of a troubled employee include, but are not necessarily limited to:

- Erratic or aggressive behavior.
- Expressions of hostility, including taking everything personally.
- Changes in performance and inconsistency in performance and behavior.
- Refusal to take direction.
- Avoiding colleagues.
- Questions and/or obsession with the grievance policy.
- Signs of depression, including slower work pace, unkempt physical appearance, expressions of despair, and inability to concentrate.
- Interest in/obsession with weapons.
- Threats of suicide.
- Belligerent or argumentative behavior.
- Perceiving self as a victim.
- Missed deadlines.
- Attendance problems.
- Mood swings.

Be a careful observer of employees' behavior and alert to changes. All of us have bad days or weeks and may snap at others or be distracted. However, a troubled employee exhibits a pattern of change, and it is those patterns of change to which you need to be observant.

Realize that many of these signs can also be indications of psychosis or other mental illnesses or signs of drug or alcohol abuse. Avoid trying to diagnose the root of the problem; just recognize that a problem exists and take appropriate action in accordance with your organization's policies, such as referring the troubled employee to the Employee Assistance Program. Of course, if there are direct threats of violence report them to the leadership—specifically human resources, legal, or security support—so appropriate action can be taken.

Perpetrators of workplace violence can be individuals other than employees or former employees. If an employee is a victim of domestic violence, the spouse or domestic partner may look to seek vengeance at your workplace. If you are aware that any of your employees are domestic violence victims or have restraining orders issued against a significant other, let the leadership in your organization know so that appropriate alerts and actions can be implemented. Of course, if one of your employees has had a restraining order issued against them it could be a sign of violent tendencies, and you should report that as well. If any of these situations exist, this would also be a good time to offer the services of the EAP to the employees.

In the unfortunate event an incident should occur in the workplace, find the closest and safest escape path. Get out, help others, prevent others from entering, and call 911 when you are safe. If you can't escape, hide (preferably behind large objects to create a barricade), lock the door and turn off lights if possible, silence cell phones, and stay quiet. The Department of Homeland Security has Active Shooter Pocket Cards that can be downloaded from its website (*www.dhs .gov/publication/active-shooter-pocket-card*) as well as other publications regarding preparedness, response, and recovery.

Question: I came from a work environment where employee burnout and turnover were high. My new organization has asked me to work on a task force to prevent employee burnout. I'm excited about the opportunity. Can you suggest some organizational-wide programs that I can propose?

Answer: It's great that your new organization wants to be proactive in preventing employee burnout and wonderful that you want to be a part of it. Preventing burnout is a responsibility that needs to be shared by the employees, managers, and leaders. Your organization is on the right path in taking a holistic approach.

There are various ways that telecommuting and flexibility can be used on a formal and informal basis. Two informal programs could be:

1. **Work from home days,** which can either be one dedicated day a week or an alternating day. Everyone can benefit from a day away from the office routine, a day of productivity, and solidarity. Even if collaboration is important to the nature of the work, time away and working alone in a controlled environment boost productivity and the quality of work.

2. **Various forms of flexible scheduling.** Staggering work hours is one way of flexible scheduling. Even on an ad-hoc basis, if a team member has an important project due, let them get it done in the comfort of home while everyone else is sitting in traffic or commuting. They will likely be more creative if they can work first then drive to the office.

In addition to workplace flexibility, make sure the organization values time off. For example, allow employees to take mental health days. If the employee knows that the organization's leadership sanctions this practice, they will be more willing to take this time off. When employees complete major projects, let them take a day off. If your business model allows, it could be a day in addition to their paid time off. If that's not possible, at least offer the opportunity to take unscheduled leave. Encourage the use of vacation days. That's what they are there for—time off. Don't be the organization that allows employees to wear their excessive time-off balances as a badge of honor.

Other things the organization can do to create a sense of balance in the workplace is to set aside space and designate it as "mindfulness space." If you have an open work space environment, this could be a quiet corner. If your work space is more traditional, perhaps a separate office could be set aside for this purpose. These spaces should be technology-free, with low lighting (lamps rather than overhead lighting), and comfortable furniture. They need not be elaborate—just quiet space where employees can get away and think.

Speaking of technology-free, consider having unplugged, organization-wide initiatives—for example, no use of technology on a certain day during certain hours. If you need to talk to someone in the same building, have a face-to-face meeting. Bonuses to this initiative are that it will help build interpersonal relationships among colleagues and will promote an environment in which people are engaged in their work and the work of their colleagues. They will want to remain in this environment and recruit their colleagues to come work for the organization as well.

Question: We're anticipating some major organizational changes soon that will impact my team. Are there things I can do now to limit the disruption to our work?

Answer: Getting a jump on change is a great idea. Anything you can do ahead of the announcement will be beneficial, but it sounds as if you already know how changes at work can be upsetting for many people.

Think about each of your employees and how they typically react to change. You probably have a few who welcome and champion change, and quickly adjust to whatever happens. These employees will be highly valuable to you and can help you sell the change to others who aren't receptive to change. Change champions are invaluable in any organizational change initiative. They will help bring others along to the best of their ability. So, if you don't know who you can count on to be a change champion, now's the time to find them.

Most likely you also have people who dig their heels in and resist any change. These employees may need special handling once the change is announced to get them on board. Others may be the kind of people who are neutral on change and wait to see how things play out before they embrace the change.

If your organization has experienced a lot of recent changes, you may find your staff is just plain tired of things always in flux. Preparing them for change can make all the difference in how effective the changes are in the long run.

Employee engagement plays a part in how ready your team is for change, so carefully monitor your team's morale. Fully engaged employees are usually more accepting of change because they're fully committed to your organization's success.

Focus more attention than usual on your organization's mission so that your team is thinking "big picture." Employees who are fully committed to your mission should be more receptive to changes designed to increase your organization's success. Talk about some of the issues the changes will impact to bring your employees up to date.

It's always important to listen to your staff, but it is critically important in times of change. Take time to hear their concerns and address those you can as quickly as you can. Your organizational grapevine will be buzzing, so head off as much as you can by being as open and transparent as possible. You can't over-communicate in times of change so plan carefully how the change will be announced and how you will follow up after the announcement.

Listen to your employees, reinforce the mission, and find your change champions. This will set the groundwork for a successful change.

Closing Thoughts

As a manager, you can expect that you'll be faced with challenging circumstances—the ones discussed in this section or others. There should be resources (internal or external) that can help you to avoid potentially perilous situations. Get to know those resources and develop relationships with the staff. Admittedly, some will never be pleasant or easy, but some will make more sense to you once you understand the rationale behind them.

Recognizing Legal Pitfalls

ADA, EEO, FMLA, ADEA, FLSA, NLRA—it's an alphabet soup of laws and regulations that an unknowing manager can trip over. In this section, we present questions about issues such as lawful interview questions, leave requirements, retaliation, union organizing activities, harassment, at-will employment, overtime and comp time, disability status, and discrimination. The answers provide guidance regarding what managers can and cannot do in certain situations and why.

Question: I've noticed employees in my department congregating during breaks, often huddled over someone's phone. I'm also overhearing talks about gatherings outside of work and comments about individual wages and task assignments. Should I mention these observations at my next staff meeting?

Answer: You have a keen awareness of what's going on with your employees, a good quality in a manager. However, in this circumstance, don't mention your observations to the employees. Rather, report this activity to senior management and/or human resources immediately. What you're witnessing could be signs of union organizing, and expert advice should be sought from legal counsel.

Under the National Labor Relations Act (NLRA), all employees have the right to organize, form, join, assist, and be represented by a union, to bargain collectively through representatives of their own choosing, and to engage in concerted activity for the purpose of mutual aid and protection such as the right to discuss terms and conditions of employment. If the employees are engaged in union organizing, or merely discussing their salaries and task assignments—a concerted activity—managers should avoid taking actions that could be considered an unfair labor practice. These actions include threatening any adverse action such as significant changes in benefits, demotions, or firing because employees are engaging in a protected activity (threats); asking employees about union activities (interrogation); suggesting or promising employment benefits, such as promotions or salary increases, if the employee will refrain from union activities (promises); or spying on union-related activities during work time and non-work time, whether on or off company premises (spying).

The path to unionization usually follows the National Labor Relations Board's process, which includes an organizing campaign (which you may be witnessing), authorization cards signed by employees expressing interest in joining the union, a petition for certification, and election campaigns and elections in which a union is or is not elected by the employees in the bargaining unit. However, recognition of a bargaining unit may occur under other circumstances, such as a union convincing the employer to grant recognition or a union convincing an employer to witness its majority status. A union may accomplish this by getting management to unintentionally count the authorization cards, thereby obligating the company to bargain with the union. Employers must be very careful granting recognition under these circumstances. Interference in this process could be considered an unfair labor practice.

Any of the employees you've noticed could be a union representative. Should they approach you directly, refrain from looking at any list of employees that a union representative attempts to give you, looking at or handling cards or letters with names on them, or accepting papers that employees attempt to hand you.

For more information, visit the National Labor Relations Board's website (*www.nlrb.gov*).

Question: I know employers can't discriminate against an employee because of certain protections, but what if an employee files a false claim or is spreading untruthful statements. Is there anything I can do?

Answer: You are correct that there are laws at the federal, state, and often local levels that protect employees from discrimination. The major federal laws include Title VII of the Civil Rights Act of 1964, which prohibits discrimination based on race, color, religion, national origin, and sex. The Age Discrimination in Employment Act prohibits discrimination against individuals over the age of forty. The Americans With Disabilities Act and its amendments prohibit discrimination against qualified individuals with physical or mental disabilities. The Equal Pay Act prohibits sex-based compensation discrimination. Employees have the right to file claims of discrimination under these laws with the Equal Employment Opportunity Commission, or EEOC.

With the exception of the Equal Pay Act, non-discrimination laws cover all terms and conditions of employment such as hiring, salary, benefits, promotions, training, performance management, termination, and discipline. Disparate treatment is a type of discrimination in which an employee is treated differently than another similarly situated employee or class because of a protected attribute.

Retaliation is a form of discrimination and an employee cannot be fired, demoted, harassed, or in any other way "retaliated against" for filing a charge of discrimination, participating in a discrimination proceeding, or otherwise opposing discrimination.

You may be tempted to take disciplinary action against the employee for filing a false discrimination claim, but that would be considered retaliation, an adverse action (discipline) taken because the employee engaged in a protected activity (filing a discrimination claim). A protected activity can also include opposition to a practice believed to be unlawful or participation in an employment discrimination proceeding, such as complaining to anyone about alleged discrimination against oneself or others, threatening to file a charge of discrimination, or refusing to obey an order reasonably believed to be discriminatory.

If the employee in question filed a claim of discrimination with the EEOC, you should not be discussing the claim with the employee. The process needs to proceed without interference. Even if the claim was filed internally within your organization, let an investigation take place. Either way, provide all of the facts you have regarding the incident or employee's concern. The purpose of either an internal or external process is to uncover all of the facts to determine what occurred.

If the employee is talking about the complaint to other members of the team and his behavior is disruptive, you should talk with senior management or your HR support. Someone other than you can reinforce with the employee the organization's expectations about workplace behavior. For more information, you can visit the EEOC's website (*www.eeoc.gov*).

Question: My organization is an at-will employer. I thought that meant an employee can be fired anytime, but I'm hearing that we have to go through lengthy discipline or performance improvement processes first. I want to be a fair manager, but I'm confused. What exactly does employment-at-will mean?

Answer: The term *employment at will* can be confusing. It means that an employee has been hired for an indefinite period of time without a written employment contract (these are usually reserved for executive staff) or under the terms of a collective bargaining agreement with a union representing the employees' interests. "At will" also means that either side—the employer or the employee—is free to terminate the employment relationship at any time and for any reason.

Over time, however, legislation has been passed at both the federal and the state levels that have strengthened employee rights (for example, Title VII of the Civil Rights Act of 1964, the Americans With Disabilities Act, and the Age Discrimination in Employment Act). These and similar laws have granted protections to employees based on certain characteristics, such as race, sex, national origin, disability status, or being over forty, and employment decisions cannot be made based on those characteristics.

Collective bargaining agreements generally require just cause for adverse employment actions. In addition to collective bargaining agreements and laws granting employees protections, employment-at-will laws vary according to state provisions and case law that have provided other exceptions including:

- **The public policy exception** prohibiting termination or other adverse action if an employee exercises a legal right (reporting an unsafe working condition, whistleblowing, or filing a discrimination claim), or an employee responds to a legal obligation (such as serving jury duty or military reserve duty).

- **The implied contract exception,** in which an employer makes statements implying job security (e.g., "Keep doing great work and you'll have a job as long as we have this contract."). The courts have found such statements as well as statements in policies and handbooks to be implied or sometimes even express contracts.

- **The covenant of good faith and fair dealing,** which prohibits an employer from engaging in actions that jeopardize or penalize an employee, such as knowingly terminating someone near retirement when it results in the denial of retirement benefits or terminating a salesman just before a large commission on a completed sale is payable.

You are right as a manager to want to treat your employees fairly. That's probably the reason that your organization has policies and protocols for discipline and performance improvement. It is never advisable to rely solely on the employment-at-will doctrine when terminating someone's employment. You should document any performance issues or difficulties an employee is experiencing and talk with the employee right away so that the issues are addressed and remedial action can be taken. If an employee is breaching the organization's code of conduct, their behavior should also be documented and addressed as soon as possible. Seek policy guidance from your organization's HR support or your manager.

Question: I have an employee who often puts in three to four hours of overtime in a week when we're working on large projects.

Rather than get paid overtime, she asks if she can take comp time when things are slower to spend time with her kids. I'd like to accommodate her request. Is there any reason I can't?

Answer: It's great that you want to support your employee's need for work-life balance. Indeed, flexible workplaces are important today. However, there are some things to consider.

The federal Fair Labor Standards Act, or FLSA, regulates the number of hours that employees can work in a workweek. Under the FLSA, the standard workweek is forty hours, and non-exempt employees in the private sector who work more hours in a workweek must receive overtime pay (time and one-half their regular pay) for every hour worked over forty. An employer has the flexibility to set the workweek as long as it is a fixed and regularly occurring period of 168 hours—seven consecutive twenty-four-hour periods. Employers in the public sector may grant compensatory time off rather than pay overtime.

Overtime is calculated based on hours actually worked and not time compensated. If a holiday occurs during the workweek for which the employee receives holiday pay, for example, those eight hours of holiday pay are not part of the forty hours worked.

You may have heard the terms *exempt employee* and *non-exempt employee*. The Department of Labor, which regulates the FLSA, generally considers all employees to be eligible for overtime, unless they meet one of the exemptions of the overtime provision. To be eligible for an exemption, an employee must satisfy the requirements of a salary-basis test and must satisfy the duties test for a particular exemption. The categories of exemptions for the duties test includes: executive, administrative, professional, highly compensated, computer employee, and outside sales. You can find more information about the FLSA by visiting the Department of Labor's website (*www.dol.gov/whd/flsa*). Of course, you should also check with internal resources in your organization such as legal or human resources, before determining if a position that an employee holds is classified exempt or non-exempt.

If the employee in your question works in a position that is classified as non-exempt, you can allow her to leave early and make up the time as long as she makes it up during the same workweek. If the time is made up in a subsequent week, you will have to pay her overtime. The FLSA's regulations are clear that an employer cannot average hours over two or more weeks.

On the other hand, if the employee is in a position that is exempt from overtime, you may grant her the flexibility she requests provided there are no internal reasons that would prevent it. Either way, you want to avoid the appearance of showing favoritism. If the non-exempt employees see their exempt peers enjoying more flexibility, they may perceive it as being unfair. You will want to communicate these differences to them so they understand that the distinction between exempt and nonexempt employees is made by law and not by the organization and that you want to ensure they, the non-exempt employees, are getting all of the protections they are entitled to receive.

Question: I just learned that one of my employees was coming in late most days while I was traveling on business. She'd been visiting her ill grandmother at the hospital. She's close with her grandmother and upset about this illness. I want to be supportive. Can I suggest she take a leave under the Family Medical Leave Act?

Answer: As a manager, it is important to recognize that situations arise in employees' personal lives that can impact work, and you should be commended for wanting to help her through a difficult time.

The Family Medical Leave Act (FMLA) provides job protected leave for up to twelve weeks to eligible employees for certain qualifying events. FMLA leave is not required to be paid, and employers can coordinate it with other types of leave such as sick leave or vacation leave.

To be eligible, the employee must work for an employer with fifty or more employees, and must have worked for at least twelve months, which need not be consecutive. (In other words, there can be breaks in employment, but the total must equal twelve months.) In addition, the employee must have worked 1,250 hours during the prior twelve months.

Qualifying events include the following:

- The birth of a child or the placement of a child for adoption.
- To care for a family member with a serious health condition. Under FMLA, a family member includes a spouse, a

parent, a child (biological, adopted, foster, step) generally under the age of 18 unless incapable of self-care because of a disability. In-laws are not included, nor are grandparents. The exception for grandparents could be if they stand or stood in loco parentis (in place of parents) when the employee was a minor.

• The employee's own health condition makes them unable to do their job.

FMLA leave is also available to qualified employees in circumstances related to a family member's call to active duty or to care for a family member who became ill or injured while on active military duty.

There are record-keeping and notice requirements to which the employer must adhere under FMLA. The employer has the right to receive notification and medical certification from the employee. Because these requirements can be extensive, it's best to work with your human resources support when employees require leave under this law.

In the situation that you described, it does not appear that your employee would be eligible for FMLA leave, unless her grandmother raised her and essentially had the role of her caretaker (stood in loco parentis) when she was a child. You should check or have her check with human resources. Your organization may offer another type of leave, such as a personal leave, that she can take under these circumstances. It might also be possible for her to work a flexible work schedule, or perhaps telecommute or work remotely part of the time, during her grandmother's hospital stay or beyond if the employee needs to provide additional care.

For more information about the FMLA, visit the Department of Labor's website (*www.dol.gov/whd/fmla*).

Question: One of my employees told me about harassment that was occurring in another department. Someone from that department confided that she was being sexually harassed, and my employee thinks the supervisor may be the culprit. I feel like I should be doing something. Should I step in or just ignore it?

Answer: Indeed, your instincts are right. When an employee complains about sexual harassment, the employer must take the complaint seriously. As a manager, there are things that you must do when you become aware of behavior that may be harassment. Whether someone tells you directly that they are being harassed, or you receive a report like the one you described, you must bring the situation forward to the appropriate individuals in your organization. If you don't you could be accountable for not taking action.

Sexual harassment is unwelcome or unwanted sexual conduct that is either very serious or occurs frequently. The harasser may be another employee, a management representative, or even a customer, and may be a male or a female harassing someone of the same or opposite sex. The conduct can be verbal, physical, written, or graphic. Behavior that creates a hostile or intimidating workplace and interferes with any employee's job performance is harassment.

The Supreme Court has said that an employer is strictly liable for a hostile work environment if the harasser is a supervisor, especially if the harassment results in a tangible employment action, such as a failure to give a raise or promotion to the employee being harassed. Even if the harasser is not a supervisor, the employer is negligent if it failed to prevent the harassment from taking place. The Equal Employment Opportunity Commission (EEOC) issued guidelines that said employers may be able to avoid or limit liability if they have policies and processes in place to prevent or promptly correct any harassing behavior. There should be a policy that prohibits harassment and provides examples of behavior and that prohibits retaliation for complaining about or reporting harassment. Further, there should be a complaint procedure and investigation process. Employers need to communicate the policy and complaint process to their employees and make it clear—through words and actions—that they will undertake immediate and corrective action if, after an investigation, behaviors are found to be harassment.

The EEOC also said that employers can show they exercise reasonable care when they advise all management staff members to address or report harassment in accordance with the organization's protocols regardless of how the manager received the information. It's not relevant if the employee followed the complaint process. Due care requires addressing and correcting harassment behaviors.

In the situation described in your question, you, a manager and representative of the company, have knowledge of some potential wrongdoing. The Courts and the EEOC are clear that if the employer knew, or should have known, then it would be difficult to have a defense. Beyond legal liability, you want to be sure that the work environment is positive. In this situation, don't get directly involved and try to talk with the employee in the other department or that employee's supervisor. Rather, report what you know to the people authorized to take the complaint and investigate it, generally your legal and/or human resources support. They are trained to deal with these issues.

Question: One of my employees was injured in an accident and will be off of work on disability leave. I'm not sure when he'll be back, but he told me he may need an accommodation when he returns. Is he covered under the Americans With Disabilities Act?

Answer: This is an area that can be confusing for managers and employees alike, so it's smart to ask this questions in advance. Not everyone who becomes sick or injured is automatically disabled, even if they take advantage of their employer's short-term or long-term disability program and benefits. Under the Americans With Disability Act (ADA), a person with a disability is someone who:

- Has a physical or mental impairment that substantially limits one or more major life activities.
- Has a record of such an impairment.
- Is regarded as having such an impairment.

A person who meets this definition has to be qualified to perform the essential functions of the job with or without a reasonable accommodation. There are a number of layers within the ADA that need to be explored with your legal and/or human resources support. For example, a major life activity is something an average person can perform with little or no difficulty, such as hearing, speaking, or breathing; or a reasonable accommodation is a modification or adjustment to a job, the work environment, or the way things are usually done; or essential job functions, which are duties or responsibilities essential to the position.

An employee who is ill or injured often may suffer limitations, even limitations to one or more major life activities. A key consideration is whether or not these limitations are short-term or permanent. Clearly, if the injury your employee suffered in the accident has caused a permanent situation that meets the ADA's definition and criteria, then the employee is covered. If he needs a reasonable accommodation, one that will not create an undue hardship on the business, then you need to provide it. Failure to do so is considered discrimination under the ADA.

Conversely, employees who go on a disability leave often do so to recover from a temporary condition or disability that is not included under the ADA. If an employee is covered by disability insurance or workers' compensation, the carrier, and the employee's physician, may want the employee to return to work as soon as possible, even on modified duty. Returning to work on a part-time basis or to limited duty has been found to help the healing process and is beneficial to the employee's recovery and well-being. When your employee suggests that he may need an accommodation, it possible that he's referring to a modified work arrangement.

Have the employee work with your legal and/or human resources support staff. They have more knowledge about what the ADA and disability programs require. It's beneficial that they get the information directly from him, rather than from you. If the employee will require some type of reasonable accommodation under the ADA, or modifications under a disability program, an integrated approach should be taken—an approach that involves legal, human resources, the employee and his healthcare providers, and you.

For more information on the ADA, visit the EEOC's website (*www.eeoc.gov/laws/statutes/ada.cfm*).

Question: Two employees from a different department have expressed interest in an available position in my department. One just turned forty-two and the other is in his late fifties. I'll interview them both, but I have reservations about the fifty-something employee. Because they are both over forty, should I be concerned with age discrimination?

Answer: Filling positions with the right person is one of the most important things a manager does. There are so many considerations, including treating everyone with fairness and respect, and avoiding unlawful discrimination against anyone. Asking this question at the beginning of the process means you are on the right path.

The Age Discrimination in Employment Act, or ADEA, makes it unlawful to discriminate against an individual on the basis of their being over the age of forty. This applies to all employment decisions, such as hiring, promoting, compensating, or terminating. Most managers do not realize that the ADEA also prohibits discriminating against individuals within the protected age group—the situation you present with two individuals over the age of forty, but one is younger. If a decision was made to hire the younger of the two because she is younger, age discrimination exists because the decision was made on the basis of her age and not qualifications to do the job. For more information on the law, visit the EEOC's website (*www.eeoc.gov /laws/statutes/adea.cfm*).

Examine your reasons for being reluctant about the older of the two candidates. The advantage of choosing among internal candidates is that you can learn more about the employment histories of each of them. Were they good performers? Were there any issues with either? What did they accomplish? Those are some of the valid pieces of information that help make an informed, unbiased decision. However, if you find yourself thinking or assuming that the older candidate will be less flexible or lack up-to-date skills, you may be letting some hidden biases into your decision-making process—an avenue for potential discrimination.

You said that you intended to interview both, and you should if they both have the qualifications of the job, for a number of reasons: First, they are both internal candidates, and it's a good employee relations practice to acknowledge their contributions and desire for potential advancement. Second, even if one has a background that appears to be stronger, the other may surprise you. There may be things you find out about him that are not evident on paper but that are revealed during your interview discussion with him. Go into both interviews with an open mind and unbiased attitude and stay focused on the job requirements.

Question: When I interview someone, I like to get to know certain things about them to make sure they will fit in with the company and the rest of the team. I understand there are some things I can't ask about. What are they and why can't I ask them?

Answer: Selecting a candidate for a job who will fit with the rest of the team is certainly important and a critical part of the hiring process, but learning job-related facts about them is most important. Employment interviews should always be focused on the position for which the individual is being considered. If you ask questions about someone's personal life, you could risk a claim of discrimination. Let's look at some questions that have potential legal pitfalls:

- "I noticed that we went to the same college. What year did you graduate?"

  Pitfall: This question has the potential to reveal the candidate's age. It's certainly okay to discuss your alma mater, but keep the questions about academics and activities related to their field of study and relevant to the job for which they are applying.

- "I see you won the B'nai B'rith Diverse Minds Youth Writing Challenge in college. Are you still involved in that organization?"

  Pitfall: This has the potential to reveal the candidate's religion, which isn't relevant to the job. It would be better to ask the candidate about their involvement only in job-related professional or technical organizations.

- "We have a great childcare facility on site. Will you need to take advantage of it?"

  Pitfall: This might be okay if you asked it of all applicants, female and male, who appear to be in an age group that may have young children. It has the potential for revealing parental and possibly marital status. Let your human resources support provide information about the organization's benefits. As a manager you have no need to know what benefits a candidate may need.

- "We have a strong team culture in this organization and team-building is ongoing. By the way, what sports do you play?"

  Pitfalls: You're assuming that the candidate plays, or even likes, sports. If you asked only men this question and not women, you would be on the brink of sex discrimination. Also, the candidate may have a disability—one that's not visible. Now you're on the edge of disability discrimination. Wanting to know how this person works on a team is a legitimate concern. It would be better to ask for examples of their experiences working with teams and the types of team-building exercises in which those teams engaged.

Questions asked during an interview should be related to the job that the individual will be performing—questions that will help you determine if the applicant has the required knowledge, skills, and, if necessary, prior experience. You can ask questions that will help determine if the individual can meet other job requirements (such as the ability to work specified work hours) or responsibilities other than work that would interfere with specific job requirements (such as traveling). This will get you the information that you will need to make an informed decision.

Closing Thoughts

The external legal and regulatory environment in which organizations have to operate is very dynamic. Laws and regulations change. Managers cannot be expected to be legal experts, but you should have an awareness of these issues so you can proceed with caution and know what to ask. The resolution of each situation that you encounter should ultimately be determined on a case-by-case basis, depending upon the particular facts. Legal counsel should be sought as appropriate.

NOTES

Section 1

1. Trent Hamm, "Warren Buffett on Reputation," The Simple Dollar website, April 18, 2008, *www.thesimpledollar.com/warren-buffett-on-reputation/.*

Section 3

1. "Third Annual Study of the State of Generation Y, Generation X, and Baby Boomers." Study by PayScale and Millennium Branding, November 19, 2014, *www.millenniumbranding.com.*
2. CareerBuilder press release, September 14, 2017.

Section 5

1. Tereza Litsa, "How Emotional Connection Increases Customer Satisfaction," ClickZ Marketing Technology Transformation website, September 15, 2016, *www.clickz.com/how-emotional-connection-increases-customer-satisfaction/105775/.*
2. Meg Marco, "Zappos Sends You Flowers," Consumerist website, October 16, 2007, *https://consumerist.com/2007/10/16/zappos-sends-you-flowers/.*

RESOURCES

Managing can be overwhelming at times and throughout this book we touched on many of the varied aspects and responsibilities of management. As comprehensive as this book is, it is impossible to discuss any one topic in depth. The following is a list of additional books that explore many of the topics we included in much greater detail.

Alda, Alan. *If I Understood You, Would I Have This Look on My Face?* (New York: Random House, 2017).

Booher, Dianna. *Communicate With Confidence* (New York: McGraw Hill, 2012).

Covey, Stephen. *7 Habits of Highly Effective People: Powerful Lessons in Personal Change* (New York: Simon & Schuster, 2013).

Eckerson, Wayne. *Performance Dashboards: Measuring, Monitoring, and Managing Your Business* (Hoboken, N.J.: John Wiley & Sons, Inc., 2010).

Fisher, Roger, William Ury, and Bruce Patton. *Getting to Yes: Negotiating Agreement Without Giving In* (New York: Penguin Books, 2011).

Goleman, Daniel. *Working With Emotional Intelligence* (New York: Bantam Books 2004).

Gostick, Adrian, and Chester Elton. *The Carrot Principle: How the Best Managers Use Recognition to Engage Their People, Retain Talent, and Accelerate Performance* (New York: Free Press, 2009).

Grazer, Brian, and Charles Fishman. *A Curious Mind: The Secret to a Bigger Life* (New York: Simon & Schuster, 2015).

Langford, Beverly. *The Etiquette Edge: Modern Manners for Business Success* (New York: AMACOM, 2016).

Leland, Karen, and Keith Bailey. *Time Management in an Instant: 60 Ways to Make the Most of Your Day* (Pompton Plains, N.J.: Career Press, 2008).

Mitchell, Barbara, and Cornelia Gamlem. *The Big Book of HR* (Wayne, N.J.: Career Press, 2017).

———. *The Conflict Resolution Phrase Book* (Wayne, N.J.: Career Press, 2017).

———. *The Essential Workplace Conflict Handbook* (Pompton Plains, N.J.: Career Press, 2015).

Nelson, Bob. *1001 Ways to Engage Employees* (Wayne, N.J.: Career Press, 2018).

Pink, Daniel H. *Drive: The Surprising Truth About What Motivates Us* (New York: Riverhead Books, a Penguin Group imprint, 2009).

GLOSSARY OF MANAGEMENT AND BUSINESS TERMS

Accident: An undesired event that results in physical harm to a person or damage to property.

Accounts Payable: Money an organization owes its vendors and suppliers.

Accounts Receivable: Money an organization's customers owe the organization.

Action Plans: Detailed steps a unit, department, or team will take to achieve short term objectives.

Active Listening: The communication technique that requires the listener to fully concentrate, understand, and respond to the speaker to ensure that messages are being related completely and properly.

Age Discrimination in Employment Act (ADEA): An act that prohibits discrimination in employment for persons age forty and over except where age is a bona fide occupational qualification.

Alternative Staffing: The use of alternative recruiting sources and workers who are not regular employees; also known as **Flexible Staffing.**

Americans With Disabilities Act (ADA): The act that prohibits discrimination against a qualified individual with a disability because of the disability of such individual.

Assets: Financial, physical, and sometimes intangible properties an organization owns.

Balance Sheet: The statement of a firm's financial position at a particular time.

Balanced Scorecard: A measurement approach that provides an overall picture of an organization's performance as measured against goals in finance, customers, internal business processes, and learning and growth.

Base Pay: The basic compensation an employee receives, usually as a wage or salary.

Behavioral Interview: A type of interview that focuses on how an applicant previously handled real work situations.

Bias: The result that occurs when an individual's values, beliefs, prejudices, or preconceived notions distort their decisions and actions.

Break-Even Analysis: Analysis that shows a point where total revenue associated with a program is equal to the total cost of the program.

Business Continuity Planning: A management process that identifies potential threats and impacts to an organization, and provides a framework for ensuring that it is able to withstand disruption, interruption, or loss of normal business functions/operation.

Capacity: The ability of an organization's operations department to yield output.

Career Development: The process by which an individual progresses through a series of stages in their careers, each of which is characterized by relatively unique issues, themes, and tasks.

Career Planning: Actions and activities that individuals perform in order to give direction to their work life.

Cause-and-Effect Diagram: A diagram that maps out a list of factors that are thought to affect a problem or a desired outcome.

Centralization: The degree to which decision-making authority is restricted to higher levels of management in an organization.

Civil Rights Act of 1991: The act that expands the possible damage awards available to victims of intentional discrimination to include compensatory and punitive damages; gives plaintiffs in cases of alleged intentional discrimination the right to a jury trial.

Closed Questions: Questions that can usually be answered with *yes* or *no*.

Coaching: On-going meetings between supervisors and employees to discuss the employee's career goals.

Code of Ethics: Principles of conduct within an organization that guide decision-making and behavior.

Collective Bargaining: The process by which management and union representatives negotiate the employment conditions for a particular bargaining unit for a designated period of time.

Collective Bargaining Agreement (CBA): An agreement or contract negotiated through collective bargaining process.

Committee: A group of people who come together for the accomplishment of a specific organizational objective.

Common Law: Dictates that custom and usage have the force of law, even if not specifically found in legislatively enacted, codified, written laws.

Competencies: The set of behaviors encompassing skills, knowledge, abilities, and personal attributes that are critical to successful work accomplishment; critical success factors needed to perform a given role in an organization.

Competency Model: The set of job competencies that together make up a profile for success for a particular job.

Compressed Workweek: A work schedule that compresses a full week's work into fewer than five days.

Constructive Confrontation: An intervention strategy that focuses on behavior and performance.

Constructive Discharge: The result that occurs when employer makes working conditions so intolerable that an employee has no choice but to resign.

Consumer Price Index (CPI): The instrument that measures change over time for costs of a group of goods and services.

Control: To an operations department, an after-the-fact evaluation of a company's ability to meet its own specifications and its customers' needs.

Cost-Benefit Analysis: A ratio that allows management to determine the financial impact particular activities and programs will have on a company's profitability.

Counseling: A form of intervention in which the emphasis is on the cause of a problem rather than on job performance.

Critical Thinking: The process of making inferences and judgments about the credibility of messages and information communicated to us.

Decentralization: The degree to which decision-making authority is given to lower levels in an organization's hierarchy.

Defamation: Injuring someone's reputation by making a false and malicious statement; may be spoken (slander) or written (libel).

Developmental Activities: Activities that focus on preparing employees for future responsibilities while increasing their capacity to perform their current jobs.

Direct Compensation: Pay that is received by an employee, including base pay, differential pay, and incentive pay.

Directive Interview: A type of interview in which the interviewer poses specific questions to a candidate and keeps control.

Disability: A physical or mental impairment that substantially limits one or more major life activities such as bathing, dressing, and so on.

Disability Benefits: Monthly benefits paid under Social Security to workers (and eligible dependents) younger than the Social Security retirement age if they have a disability.

Disaster Recovery Plan: Guidelines and procedures to be used by an organization for the recovery of data lost due to severe forces of nature, such as earthquakes, fires, tornadoes, floods, or hurricanes.

Disparate Impact: The result that occurs when the selection rate for a protected class (protected under non-discrimination laws) is significantly less than the rate for the class with the highest selection rate; also known as adverse impact.

Disparate Treatment: The result that occurs when protected classes are intentionally treated differently from other employees or are evaluated by different standards.

Distance Learning: The process of delivering educational or instructional programs to locations away from a classroom or site.

Diversity: Differences in characteristics of people; can involve personality, work style, race, age, ethnicity, gender, religion, education, functional level at work, and so on.

Duty of Good Faith and Fair Dealing: The imposition on each party in a contract an obligation for honesty in the conduct of the transaction.

E-Learning: The delivery of formal and informal training and educational materials, processes, and programs via the use of electronic media.

Emotional Intelligence (EI): The ability of an individual to be sensitive to and understanding of the emotions of others and to manage their own emotions and impulses.

Employee Assistance Programs (EAPs): Company-sponsored programs that deliver a variety of health-related services, which are provided by licensed professionals or organizations and offer employees a high degree of confidentiality.

Employment Branding: The process of positioning an organization as an "employer of choice" in the labor market.

Employment Offer: The formal process that makes the hiring decision official; should immediately follow the final decision to hire a candidate; formally communicated through offer letter.

Employment-at-Will: The common-law principle stating that employers have the right to hire, fire, demote, and promote whomever they choose for any reason unless there is a law or contract to the contrary and that employees have the right to quit a job at any time.

Environmental Scanning: The process that surveys and interprets relevant data to identify external opportunities and threats.

Equal Employment Opportunity Commission (EEOC): The federal agency responsible for enforcing non-discrimination laws and handling alleged complaints.

Equal Pay Act (EPA): The act that prohibits wage discrimination by requiring equal pay for equal work.

Equity: The amount of owners' or shareholders' portion of a business.

Essential Function: A primary job duty that a qualified individual must be able to perform, either with or without accommodation; a function may be considered essential because it is required in a job or because it is highly specialized.

Ethics: A system of moral principles and values that establish appropriate conduct.

Executive Search Firms: External recruiting method; firms seek out candidates, usually for executive, managerial, or professional positions.

Exempt Employees: Employees who are excluded from the Fair Labor Standards Act overtime pay requirements.

Extrinsic Rewards: Rewards such as pay, benefits, bonuses, promotions, achievement awards, time off, more freedom and autonomy, special assignments, and so on.

Fair Labor Standards Act (FLSA): The act that regulates employee overtime status, overtime pay, child labor, minimum wage, record-keeping, and other administrative concerns.

Family and Medical Leave Act (FMLA): The act that provides employees with up to twelve weeks of unpaid leave to care for family members or because of a serious health condition of the employee.

First-Impression Error: A type of interviewer bias in which an interviewer makes snap judgments and lets first impressions (either positive or negative) cloud the interview.

Flexible Staffing: The use of alternative recruiting sources and workers who are not regular employees; also known as **Alternative Staffing.**

Flextime: A work schedule that requires employees to work an established number of hours per week but allows starting and ending times to vary.

Formula Budgeting: The form of budgeting in which an average cost is applied to comparable expenses and general funding is changed by a specific amount.

Fraudulent Misrepresentation: The intentional deception relied upon and resulting in injury to another person.

Functional Structure: An organizational structure that defines departments by what services they contribute to the organization's overall mission.

Gantt Chart: A project-planning tool that graphically displays activities of a project in sequential order and plots them against time.

Generation X: The group of people born roughly between the years of 1965 and 1980.

Generation Z: The group of people born roughly between 1997 and 2014.

Goal: A clear statement, usually in one sentence, of the purpose and intent of a department, a project, or a program.

Gross Domestic Product (GDP): The estimate of the total value of goods and services produced in a country in a given year.

Gross Profit Margin: The measure of the difference between what it costs to produce a product and the selling price.

Group Interview: A type of interview in which multiple job candidates are interviewed by one or more interviewers at the same time or where multiple people in an organization interview a single job candidate.

Halo Effect: A type of interviewer bias in which interviewer allows one strong point in a candidate's favor to overshadow all other information.

Horn Effect: A type of interviewer bias in which the interviewer allows one strong point that works against candidate to overshadow all other information.

Hostile Environment Harassment: A type of harassment that occurs when sexual or other discriminatory conduct is so severe and pervasive that it interferes with an individual's performance; creates an intimidating, threatening, or humiliating work environment; or perpetuates a situation that affects the employee's psychological well-being.

Human Capital: The combined knowledge, skills, and experience of a company's employees.

Implied Contract: Exists when an agreement is implied from circumstances even though there is no express agreement between employer and employee.

In Loco Parentis ("in place of a parent"): The term used in expansion of FMLA coverage to employees who stand in place of a parent with day-to-day responsibilities to care for and financially support a child or who have a day-to-day responsibility to care for or financially support a person who stood in loco parentis for them.

Incentive Pay: A form of direct compensation in which employers pay for performance beyond normal expectations to motivate employees to perform at higher levels.

Incident: Any deviation from an acceptable standard.

Income Statement: The financial statement explaining revenues, expenses, and profits over a specified period of time, usually a year or a quarter.

Incremental Budgeting: The form of budgeting in which the prior budget is the basis for allocation of funds.

Indirect Compensation: A form of compensation commonly referred to as benefits.

Internal Equity: The result that occurs when people feel that performance or job differences result in corresponding differences in pay rates.

Intrinsic Rewards: Meaningful work, good feedback on performance, autonomy, and other factors that lead to high levels of satisfaction in the job.

Inventory: To an operations department, an organization's major asset after physical buildings and equipment.

Involuntary Termination: The type of termination that occurs when employers discharge particular employees for cause (e.g., poor performance or violations of employer policy).

Job Analysis: The systematic study of jobs to determine what activities and responsibilities they include, relative importance and relationship with other jobs, personal qualifications necessary for performance of jobs, and conditions under which work is performed.

Job Burnout: The depletion of physical/mental resources caused by excessive striving to reach an unrealistic work-related goal.

Job Description: A summary of the most important features of a job, including required tasks, knowledge, skills, abilities, responsibilities, and reporting structure.

Knowledge: One's level of learning characterized by ability to recall specific facts.

Leadership: The ability of an individual to influence a group or another individual toward the achievement of goals and results.

Learning Organization: An organization characterized by a capability to adapt to changes in environment.

Learning Styles: Ways individuals learn and process ideas.

Liabilities: An organization's debts and other financial obligations.

Lifelong Learning: The ongoing pursuit of knowledge for either personal or professional gain.

Long-Term Objectives: The specific results, accomplished in three to five years, that an organization seeks to achieve in pursuing its mission.

Management: Those individuals who direct day-to-day organizational operations.

Marketing: The process of planning, pricing, promoting, and distributing goods and services to satisfy organizational objectives.

Matrix Structure: An organizational structure that combines departmentalization by division and function to gain the benefits of both.

Mediation: The method of nonbinding dispute resolution involving a third party who helps disputing parties reach a mutually agreeable decision; also known as **conciliation.**

Mentoring: A developmentally oriented relationship between two individuals.

Merit Pay: A situation in which an individual's performance is the basis for either the amount or timing of pay increases; also called **performance-based pay.**

Millennials: The group of people born roughly between the years 1981 and 1997. Also known as **Generation Y.**

Mission Statement: A statement that specifies what the company does, who its customers are, and the priorities it has set in pursuing its work.

Motivation: Factors that initiate, direct, and sustain human behavior over time.

National Labor Relations Act (NLRA): The act that protects the rights of employees to organize unhampered by management; also known as **Wagner Act.**

National Labor Relations Board (NLRB): The agency that has authority to conduct union representation elections and investigate unfair labor practices.

Needs Assessment: A process by which an organization's needs are identified in order to help the organization accomplish its objectives; also called needs analysis.

Negligent Hiring: The hiring of an employee who the employer knew or should have known, based on a reasonable pre-hire investigation of the employee's background, posed a risk to others in the workplace.

Negligent Retention: The retention of employees who engage in misconduct both during and after working hours.

Nondirective Interview: A type of interview in which interviewer asks open questions and provides general direction but allows applicant to guide process.

Nonexempt Employees: Employees covered under FLSA regulations, including overtime pay requirements.

Occupational Illness: A medical condition or disorder, other than one resulting from an occupational injury, caused by exposure to environmental factors associated with employment.

Occupational Injury: An injury that results from a work-related accident or exposure involving a single incident in the work environment.

Occupational Safety and Health Act (OSHA): The act that established the first national policy for safety and health and continues to deliver standards that employers must meet to guarantee the health and safety of their employees.

Occupational Safety and Health Administration (OSHA): The agency that administers and enforces the Occupational Safety and Health Act of 1970.

Offer Letter: A document that formally communicates the employment offer, making the hiring decision official.

Older Workers Benefit Protection Act (OWBPA): The act that amended the Age Discrimination in Employment Act to include all employee benefits; also provided terminated employees with time to consider group termination or retirement programs and consult an attorney.

On-Boarding: The process of new employee integration into the organization; often lasts up to six months or a year.

On-the-Job Training (OJT): The training provided to employees at the work site utilizing demonstration and performance of job tasks to be accomplished.

Open-Ended Question: A question that can't be answered with a *yes* or *no* (for example, "Tell me about how you _____.").

Organizational Culture: Shared attitudes and perceptions in an organization.

Organizational Development (OD): The process of enhancing the effectiveness of an organization and the well-being of its members through planned interventions.

Organizational Exit: The process of managing the way people leave an organization.

Organizational Learning: Certain types of learning activities or processes that may occur at any one of several levels in an organization.

Organizational Unit: Any discrete component of an organization in which there is a level of supervision responsible and accountable for the selection, compensation, and so on, of employees within the unit.

Orientation: The initial phase of employee training that covers job responsibilities and procedures, organizational goals and strategies, and company policies.

Outplacement: A systematic process by which a laid-off or terminated employee is counseled in the techniques of career self-appraisal and in securing a new job that is appropriate to their talents and needs.

Outsourcing: A flexible staffing option in which an independent company with expertise in operating a specific function contracts with a company to assume full operational responsibility for the function.

Overtime Pay: The required pay for nonexempt workers under FLSA at one-and-a-half times the regular rate of pay for hours worked over forty hours in a workweek.

Panel Interview: A type of interview in which structured questions are spread across a group; the individual who is most competent in the relevant area usually asks the question.

Patterned Interview: A type of interview in which the interviewer asks each applicant questions that are from the same knowledge, skill, or ability area; also called a **Targeted Interview.**

Performance Appraisal: A process that measures the degree to which an employee accomplishes work requirements.

Performance Management: The process of maintaining or improving employee job performance through the use of performance assessment tools, coaching, and counseling as well as providing continuous feedback.

Performance Standards: Expectations of management translated into behaviors and results that employees can deliver.

Policy: A broad statement that reflects an organization's philosophy, objectives, or standards concerning a particular set of management or employee activities.

Positional Negotiation: The type of negotiation in which people lock themselves into positions and find it difficult to move away, parties lose sight of the underlying problems to be resolved, and emphasis is placed on winning the position.

Prescreening Interview: A type of interview that is useful when an organization has a high volume of applicants for a job and face-to-face interviews are needed to judge prequalification factors.

Principled Negotiation: The type of contract negotiation based on four premises: 1) separate the people from the problem, 2) focus on interests, not positions, 3) invent options for mutual gain, and 4) insist on objective criteria.

Procedure: A detailed, step-by-step description of the customary method of handling an activity.

Process-Flow Analysis: A diagram of the steps involved in a process.

Product: What an organization sells to make a profit.

Program Evaluation Review Technique (PERT) Chart: A project management tool used to schedule, organize, and coordinate tasks within a project.

Progressive Discipline: A system of increasingly severe penalties for employee discipline.

Project: A series of tasks and activities that has a stated goal and objectives, a schedule with defined start and end dates, and a budget that sets limits on the use of monetary and human resources.

Project Team: A group of people who come together for a specific project.

Proprietary Information: Sensitive information owned by a company that gives the company certain competitive advantages.

Protected Class: People who are covered under a federal or state discrimination law; groups protected by EEO designations include women, African-Americans, Hispanics, Native Americans, Asian-Americans, people age forty or older, the disabled, veterans, and religious groups.

Qualitative Analysis: Analysis based on research that uses open-ended interviewing to explore and understand attitudes, opinions, feelings, and behavior.

Quantitative Analysis: Analysis that seeks to obtain easily quantifiable data on a limited number of measurement points.

Quid Pro Quo Harassment: A type of sexual harassment that occurs when an employee is forced to choose between giving in to a superior's sexual demands and forfeiting an economic benefit such as a pay increase, a promotion, or continued employment.

Reasonable Accommodation: Modifying the job application process, work environment, or circumstances under which job is performed to enable a qualified individual with a disability to be considered for the job and perform its essential functions.

Regulation: A rule or order issued by a government agency; often has the force of law.

Request for Proposal (RFP): A written request asking contractors to propose solutions and prices that fit a customer's requirements.

Resume: A document prepared by job candidate (or a professional hired by a candidate) to highlight a candidate's strengths and experience.

Retaliatory Discharge: A result of an employer punishing an employee for engaging in activities protected by the law (e.g., filing a discrimination charge or opposing unlawful employer practices).

Retention: The ability to keep talented employees in an organization.

Return on Investment (ROI): A calculation that compares the money earned (or lost) on an investment to the amount of money being invested.

Reverse Mentoring: The practice of pairing older workers with younger ones so they can educate each other (rather than the mentor always being the older worker).

Risk Management: The use of insurance and other strategies in an effort to prevent or minimize an organization's exposure to liability in the event a loss or injury occurs.

Safety: Freedom from hazard, risk, or injury.

Safety Committees: Committees composed of workers from different levels and departments who are involved in safety planning and programs.

Salary: A uniform amount of money paid to a worker regardless of how many hours are worked.

Sales: The business function responsible for selling an organization's product to the marketplace.

Scheduling: To an operations department, the act of detailed planning; based upon incoming orders, order history, and forecasts of future demand.

Security: Physical/procedural measures used to protect people, property, and information in the workplace.

Selection: The process of hiring the most suitable candidate for a vacant position.

Selection Interview: An interview designed to probe areas of interest to interviewer in order to determine how well a job candidate meets the needs of the organization.

Seniority: A system that shows preference to employees with the longest service.

Serious Health Condition: As defined in the FMLA, a condition that requires inpatient hospital, hospice, or residential care or continuing physician care.

Sexual Harassment: Unwelcome sexual advances, requests for sexual favors, and other verbal or physical conduct of a sexual nature.

Short-Term Disability (STD) Coverage: Coverage that replaces a portion of lost income for a specified period of time for employees who are ill or have nonwork-related injuries.

Short-Term Objectives: Milestones that must be achieved, usually within six months to one year, in order to reach long-term objectives.

Sick Leave: A specified period of time during which employees who are ill or have non-work-related injuries receive their full salary.

Span of Control: A reference to the number of individuals who report to a supervisor.

Staff Units: Work groups that assist line units by performing specialized services, such as human resources, finance, procurement, or legal.

Staffing: The function that identifies organizational human capital needs and attempts to provide an adequate supply of qualified individuals for jobs in an organization.

Standards: For an operations department, the yardstick by which the amount and quality of output are measured.

Stereotyping: The type of interviewer bias that involves forming generalized opinions about how people of a given gender, religion, or race appear, think, act, feel, or respond.

Strategic Management: Processes and activities used to formulate business objectives, practices, and policies.

Strategic Planning: The art and science of formulating, developing, implementing, and evaluating cross-functional decisions that enable an organization to achieve its objectives.

Strategic Thinking: The process in which people think about, assess, view, and create the future for themselves and others.

Strategies: The methods that provide the direction that enables an organization to achieve its long-term objectives.

Stress: A mental and physical condition that results from a real or perceived threat and the inability to remove it or cope with it.

Stress Interview: A type of interview in which interviewer assumes an aggressive posture to see how a candidate responds to stressful situations.

Structured Interview: A type of interview in which interviewer asks every applicant the same questions; also called a **Repetitive Interview.**

Succession Planning: The process of systematically identifying, assessing, and developing leadership talent.

Supply Chain: A global network used to deliver products and services from raw materials to end customers through an engineered flow of information, physical distribution, and cash.

SWOT Analysis: A vehicle for collecting information on an organization's current strengths, weaknesses, opportunities, and threats.

Talent Management: Systems designed to develop processes for attracting, developing, retaining, and utilizing people with the required skills and aptitude to meet current and future business needs.

Targeted Interview: A type of interview in which interviewer asks each applicant questions that are from the same knowledge, skill, or ability area; also called a **Patterned Interview.**

Team Interview: A type of interview used in situations in which the position relies heavily on team cooperation; supervisors, subordinates, and peers are usually part of the process.

Telecommuting: Working via computing and telecommunications equipment.

Title VII of the Civil Rights Act of 1964: The act that prohibits discrimination or segregation based on race, color, national origin, religion, and gender in all terms and conditions of employment.

Total rewards: All forms of financial returns that employees receive from their employers.

Training: The process of providing knowledge, skills, and abilities (KSAs) specific to a task or job.

Transformational Leadership: A leadership style that motivates employees by inspiring them to join in a mutually satisfying achievement.

Turnover: An annualized formula that tracks number of separations and total number of workforce employees for each month.

Union: Formal association of employees that promotes the interests of its membership through collective action.

Values: A set of principles that describes what is important to an organization, dictates employee behavior, and creates the organization's culture.

Vicarious Liability: The legal doctrine under which a party can be held liable for the wrongful actions of another party.

Virtual Organization: A short-term alliance between independent organizations in a potentially long-term relationship to design, produce, and distribute a product.

Vision Statement: A vivid, guiding image of an organization's desired future.

Wellness Programs: Preventive health programs offered by employers designed to improve the health and physical well-being of employees both on and off the job.

Workforce Planning: The process an organization uses to analyze its current base of employees and determine steps it must take to prepare for future skill and labor needs.

Work-Related Disability: A physical condition (accident or illness) that is caused, aggravated, precipitated, or accelerated by work activity or the work environment.

Workweek: Any fixed, recurring period of 168 hours (7 days x 24 hours = 168 hours).

ABOUT THE AUTHORS

In 2010, Career Press approached Barbara Mitchell about writing another book. She had previously coauthored *The Essential HR Handbook* with Sharon Armstrong. When the proposal was accepted, Barbara reached out to her colleague Cornelia Gamlem with the offer to coauthor *The Big Book of HR*. Drawing on their collective experience, Barbara and Cornelia produced a great resource for HR professionals, managers, business leaders, and small-business owners—anyone who has to manage people. A writing partnership was born. Since the publication of *The Big Book of HR*, Barbara and Cornelia have written *The Essential Workplace Conflict Handbook* and *The Conflict Resolution Phrase Book*. They also collaborate on a weekly blog, *Making People Matter*. They are likely to write more books in the future.

Both Barbara and Cornelia are influencers to the business and HR communities. They are frequent speakers to business groups and have been quoted in major publications including the *Wall Street Journal, Financial Times, Fortune, New York Times, Forbes, CEO Magazine, Globe & Mail, Fast Company, Chicago Tribune, Newsday, New York Post,* and *HR Magazine.* They have been interviewed in major markets around the country and contributed articles to numerous blogs and websites, including fastcompany.com, forbes.com, INC.com, *CEOWorld Magazine,* Entrepreneur.com, ChiefExecutive.net, and TrainingIndustry.com.

Barbara Mitchell is an author, a speaker, and the managing partner of The Mitchell Group, a human resources and organizational development consulting practice. She consults with a wide variety of clients on issues around people—helping them successfully hire, develop, engage, and retain the best talent available. Most of her HR career was spent in senior leadership positions with Marriott International, Human Genome Sciences, and as co-owner and principal of The Millennium Group, LLC.

She entered the HR profession after gaining a strong business foundation and says, "Working in HR was like coming home. I'd found what I was meant to do!"

Barbara has actively given back to the HR profession in a variety of ways. She served on the board of directors of the Employment Management Association and has been president of several SHRM chapters.

She is graduate of North Park University (Chicago, Illinois), with a degree in history and political science. She has taken graduate level business courses at UCLA, the University of Denver, and Loyola University.

Barbara is a video presenter/docent at the Smithsonian's American Art Museum and is a past member of the executive committee of the board of directors of the Northern Virginia Habitat for Humanity affiliate. She resides in the Washington, DC, metro area.

Cornelia Gamlem, SPHR, is an author, consultant, and speaker. She is founder and president of the Gems Group, a management consulting firm that offers human resources and business solutions. Prior to her consulting career, she served in a senior HR leadership role with a Fortune 500 IT services company with a global presence. She likes to say that she's been in HR since "God was a girl."

Cornelia has served on national task forces that influenced public policy and testified before the Equal Employment Opportunity Commission on three occasions. She served on SHRM's national board of directors and Global Forum board of directors, and chaired its workplace diversity committee. She has supported HR professionals by serving as an instructor at number of colleges in the Washington, DC metro area. She has written many articles and white papers for professional and industry publications. She has also served as a technical editor for McGraw Hill Education.

She is a graduate of Marymount University, from which she earned a master's degree in human resource management and California State University, Sacramento, from which she earned her undergraduate degree in business administration. She achieved Life Certification as Senior Professional in Human Resources (SPHR) from the Human Resource Certification Institute (HRCI). Cornelia resides in Albuquerque, New Mexico.

Stay Connected with Barbara and Cornelia

Visit our websites:
www.bigbookofhr.com
www.essentialworkplaceconflicthandbook.com

Read our weekly blog:
makingpeoplematter.blogspot.com

Follow us on Twitter:
@bigbookofhr
@gotworkconflict

Other Books by These Authors:
Barbara Mitchell and Cornelia Gamlem:
The Big Book of HR
The Essential Workplace Conflict Handbook
The Conflict Resolution Phrase Book

Barbara Mitchell and Sharon Armstrong:
The Essential HR Handbook

If this book or any of our others were useful tools for you, we'd be honored if you'd post a great review on Amazon.